Vital Record of Rhode Island.

1636=1850.

FIRST SERIES.

BIRTHS, MARRIAGES AND DEATHS.

A Family Register for the People.

By James N. Arnold,

EDITOR OF THE NARRAGANSETT HISTORICAL REGISTER.

"Is My Name Written in the Book of Life?"

Volume 4.   **MIDDLETOWN.**   **Part III.**

Published under the Auspices of the General Assembly.

PROVIDENCE, R. I:
NARRAGANSETT HISTORICAL PUBLISHING COMPANY.
1893.

Notice

In many older books, foxing (or discoloration) occurs and, in some instances, print lightens with wear and age. Reprinted books, such as this, often duplicate these flaws, notwithstanding efforts to reduce or eliminate them. The pages of this reprint have been digitally enhanced and, where possible, the flaws eliminated in order to provide clarity of content and a pleasant reading experience.

Vital Record of Rhode Island 1636-1850: Middletown

Originally published:
Providence, Rhode Island
1893

Reprinted by

Janaway Publishing, Inc.
732 Kelsey Ct.
Santa Maria, California 93454
(805) 925-1038
www.janawaygenealogy.com

1999, 2015

ISBN: 978-1-59641-023-7

Made in the United States of America

AN ACT INCORPORATNG THE TOWN OF MIDDLETOWN.

General Assembly at Newport, June 13, 1743.

AN ACT for dividing the town of Newport, in the county of Newport, into two towns.

Be it enacted by the General Assembly of this colony, and by the authority thereof, it is enacted, that the said town of Newport be divided into two towns, and the division to begin at the head of the creek that separates the two farms of the Hon. Joseph Whipple, Esq., and Godfrey Malbone of said Newport, merchant, and so to extend upon a direct line between the two houses of Elisha Card and that in the possession of Samuel Pemberton, Esq.; and from thence on a straight line to the place where the creek on Easton's Beach runs into the sea, and all to the southward and westward of the said line to belong to the town of Newport, and all to the northward and eastward of said line to be incorporated into a town by the name of Middletown.

And be it further enacted by the authority aforesaid that John Dexter, Esq., Messrs. Benjamin Peckham, Jr., and Sam'l Easton, surveyor, be, and they are hereby appointed a committee, they, or the major part of them, to run the aforesaid line and make report to the next session of this Assembly.

(R. I. Colonial Records, Vol. V. page 66.)

In General Assembly at Newport, 4th Tuesday in August, 1743.

AN ACT for incorporating the northeast part of the town of Newport into a township and the same to be distinguished and known by the name of Middletown.

Whereas, the General Assembly, at their session held by adjournment at Newport, within and for said colony, on the 2d Monday in June, last past, did, among other things, enact that the town of Newport should be divided into two towns; and for that purpose appointed a committee to run the dividing line, and make report thereon to this present session of the Assembly, who have accordingly reported that they have done the same in the following manner:

"Beginning at the head of the creek that separates the two farms of the Hon. Joseph Whipple, Esq., and Godfrey Malbone, of said Newport, merchant, and on a south course, nineteen degrees and a half east run a straight lint extending to the southwest corner of a lot of land belonging to Joh Almy of said Newport, merchant; the said corner being between the houses of Elisha Card, and that in the possession of Samuel Pemberton; and from said corner, a straight line south twenty-seven degrees east, crossing the bridge that lieth over the creek on Easton's Beach, and into the sea on that course, it being the place where the said creek usually runs into the sea."

And the said report being excepted:

Be it enacted by the General Assembly of this colony, and by the authority of the same it is enacted, that all the lands to the southward and westward of the said line, as beforedescribed, belong to the town of Newport; and that all the lands to the northward and eastward of said line be distinguished and known by the name of Midletown; and that the inhabitants of said Middletown, from time to time, shall have and enjoy the like benefits, liberties, privileges and immunities with other towns in this colony, according to charter.

And be it further enacted by the authority aforesaid, that the Justices of the Peace, living within the aforesaid town of Middletown, shall remain and continue in their aforesaid offices until the next General Election, and that the first of said Justices of the Peace grant forth his warrant to call the inhabitants of said Middletown together on Tuesday next, being the 30th day of August instant, to elect and appoint such town officers as they shall have occasion for, and as the law directs; and to appoint the time and places of their town meetings; and to choose and elect two Deputies to represent them at the next General Assembly, and so on, as by the charter is directed.

And be it further enacted by the authority aforesaid, that said town of Middletown shall send one grand and three petit jurors to the Superior Court of Judicature, Court of Assize and General Jail Delivery, and three grand and three petit jurors to every Inferior Court of Common Pleas and General Sessions of the Peace held within the county of Newport; and that the town of Newport shall hereafter send to each of the aforesaid Courts so many jurors less of what they are now compelled by law, as is ordered to be sent by the aforesaid town of Middletown.

(R. I. Colonial Records, Vol. V., pages 68-70.)

MIDDLETOWN.

MARRIAGES.

A

69   ALBRO David, Jr., of David, of Middletown, and Phebe Sisson, of George of Portsmouth; m. by Elder William Bliss, Oct. 13, 1796.

155   "   Susan B., and Joseph Barker, July 18, 1841.

10   ALLEN Samuel, and Mary Coggeshall; m. by Gideon Cornell, Asst., Jan. 16, 1745.

12   "   Rachel, and Thomas Cornell, Oct. 16, 1746.

55   "   Rowland, and Sarah Sheldon; m. by William Stoddard, Justice, Dec. 28, 1769.

79   "   William, of Peleg and Elizabeth and Lucy Little, of Fobes and Sarah; m. at Little Compton, by Rev. Jonathan Ellis, Aug. 12, 1781.

101   "   Elisha, of Middletown, and Lydia Beebe, of Newport; m. by Joseph Peabody, Justice, Sept. 21, 1783.

88   "   John, of Samuel, of Middletown, and Hannah Cook, of George, of Tiverton; m. by Walter Cook, Justice, April 26, 1784.

92   "   Hannah, and James Dyer, Jr., June 7, 1792.

80   "   Abigail, and Benjamin Howland, Jr., Dec. 22, 1799.

88   "   Benjamin, of South Kingstown, son of Christopher and Susanna Allen, of Thomas, of Middletown; m. by Rev. Michael Eddy, Dec. 2, 1804.

88   "   Susanna, and Benjamin Allen, Dec. 2, 1804.

177   "   Benjamin, of Elisha of Middletown, and Susanna Hunt, of John, of Portsmouth; m. by Thomas Cory, Justice, Feb. 11, 1808.

116   "   Samuel, and Henrietta Gould; m. by Rev. Samuel Towle, Aug. 4, 1814.

162   "   Deborah, and Joshua Coggeshall, Nov. 26, 1815.

158   "   William C., of George and Bathana C. Wyatt of Nathaniel; m. by Rev. James Taylor, Dec. 29, 1836.

96   ALMY Holder, of Job, and Elizabeth Card, of Richard; m. by Rev. William Culver, Nov. 7, 1799.

104   "   Samuel, of Job, of Newport, and Phebe Irish, of George, dec., of Middletown; m., by Rev. Michael Eddy, Nov. 12, 1801.

161   "   Benjamin, of Andrew, and Harriet Barker, of Arnold; m. by Rev. James Taylor, Nov. 17, 1839.

123   ANTHONY Richard, of Daniel, of Middletown, and Sarah Lawton, of Giles, of Portsmouth; m., by Rev. Michael Eddy, Oct. 1, 1801.

107   "   Jonathan, of Gould, of Middletown, and Rachel Church, of Caleb, of Little Compton; m. by Rev. Michael Eddy, Oct. 27, 1805.

128   "   Philip, of Gideon, and Mary Manchester, of John; m., by Rev. Michael Eddy, Dec. 4, 1817.

120   "   Abbie, and Joshua Anthony, Oct. 14, 1821.

120   "   Joshua, of Middletown, and Abbie Anthony, of Portsmouth; m. by Rev. William Patten, Oct. 14, 1821.

137   "   Sarah, and John P. Coggeshall, Oct. 9, 1823.

126   "   Rhoda, and Robert C. Sisson, Setp. 5, 1824.

132   "   Silvester, and Thomas C. Wyatt, Mar. 13, 1825.

136   "   Charles, of Portsmouth, son of Abraham and Mary, and Patience Perry, of Tiverton, dau. of Bleecker and Hannah; m. by Edmund Estes, Justice, Feb. 17, 1828.

17 ANTUNES Joseph, and Content Bliss; m. by Edward Easton, Justice, July 10, 1750.

B

1-46 BAILEY Sarah, and Joshua Coggeshall, Jan. 12, 1743-4.
35 " William, and Hannah Easton; m. by Rev. Nicholas Eyres, July 12, 1757.
61 " Ruth, and Edward Chapman, Nov. 7, 1765.
61 " Samuel, and Mary Ryder; m. by Rev. Gardiner Thurston, June 7, 1769.
145 " Mrs. Mary, and William Slocum, May 30, 1785.
56 " Easton, and Mary Irish; m. by Rev. Gardiner Thurston, March 16, 1788.
117 " Sarah C., and David Coggeshall, March 12, 1851.
2 BARKER Robert, and Phebe Smith, both of Newport; m. by Peleg Smith, Justice, Oct. 25, 1733.
45 " John, and Rebecca ——, Sept. 25, 1735.
6 " John, of Newport, and Rebecca Hoar, of said place; m. by Peleg Smith, Justice, Sept. 25, 1735.
5 " Robert, and Sarah Hoar, both of Newport; m. by John Gardiner, Justice, April 20, 1738.
20 " Deborah, and Hezekiah Hoar, Sept. 14, 1738.
4 " William, Jr., and Mary Slocum; m. by Daniel Gould, Justice, Nov. 5, 1744.
14 " James, of James, Jr., and Mrs. Ann Peckham; m. by Rev. William Vinall, Jan. 5, 1748.
43 " James, Jr., and Anne Peckham; m. by Rev. William Vinall, Jan. 5, 1748-9.
24 " Robert, of Middletown, and Frances Sanford, of Portsmouth; m. by Daniel Gould, Justice, Feb. 15, 1753.
42 " Giles, and Mary Tew; m. by Elder Gardiner Thurston, April 13, 1760.
53 " Elisha, of John and Phebe Peckham, of William; m. by Edward, Upham, Justice, Nov. 8, 1767.
58 " James, 3d, of Middletown, and Rhoda Mason, of Swansey; m. by Elder Job Mason, Aug. 16, 1770.
68 " David, of Middletown, and Mrs. Eunice Sherman, of Portsmouth; m. by Rev. Gardiner Thurston, Oct. 1, 1772.
71 " Isaac, and Sarah Peckham; m. by Rev. Gardiner Thurston, Dec. 2, 1775.
96 " Samuel, and Sarah Smith; m. by Rev. Gardiner Thurston, April 26, 1781.
91 " Gideon, and Elizabeth Croade; m. by Rev. Gardiner Thurston, Oct. 25, 1781.
115 " Peleg, of Peter and Ruth, and Mary Ward, of Richard and Elizabeth, June 3, 1784.
64 " Benjamin, of Middletown, and Mary Robertson, of Portsmouth; m. by Joseph Peabody, Justice, Feb. 18, 1789.
73 " Levi, of Middletown, and Rebecca Kempton, of New Bedford; m. by Edward Pope, Justice, May 12, 1793.
100 " Rebecca, and George Smith, Nov. 23, 1796.
104 " Mary, and Benjamin T. Sheffield, Dec. 10, 1801.
114 " Sarah, and Asa Coggeshall, Feb. 21, 1802.
112 " Giles, of Matthew, of Middletown, and Lillas Sanford, of Peleg, of Tiverton; m. by Rev. Michael Eddy, Oct. 23, 1803.
111 " Nathaniel, of Gideon, and Mary Peckham, of Peleg; m. by Rev. Michael Eddy, Dec. 1, 1803.
139 " Dorcas, and John Barker, April 20, 1805.
139 " John, and Dorcas Barker; m. by Rev. Michael Eddy, April 20, 1805.
121 " Cynthia, and Gideon Peckham, Jan. 2, 1806.
85 " Catherine, and Daniel Peckham, Nov. 2, 1806.
92 " Mary, a ... edde Clarke, Jan. 15, 1807.

126   BARKER Sarah, and J. Bailey Hall, Nov. 22, 1810.
86   "   Joseph, of Middletown, and Esther Peckham, of Newport; m. by Rev. John B. Gibson, Jan. 16, 1814.
140   "   James, of Isaac, and Ruth Wilcox, of Abner; m. by Rev. Michael Eddy, May 5, 1814.
112   "   Eleazer, of David and Lydia Sanford, of Peleg; m. by Rev. Michael Eddy, Feb. 16, 1816.
151   "   John C., and Mary Taylor; m. by Rev. Michael Eddy, March 1, 1832.
154   "   Eliphal, and James Barker, May 23, 1833.
154   "   James, of Isaac and Sarah, and Eliphal Barker, of Peleg and Sally; m. by Rev. Elijah Macumber, May 23, 1833.
151   "   Isaac, and Wealthy Peckham; m. by Rev. Michael Eddy, June 23, 1833.
167   "   Job M., of John and Julia M. Sherman, of Jacob; m. by Rev. James Taylor, May 3, 1837.
159   "   Mary, and Charles B. Davis, Feb. 22, 1839.
160   "   Ann, and William T. Wyatt, March 31, 1839.
160   "   Arnold M., of Peter, of Middletown, and Mary H. Gifford, of Judith, of Freetown; m. by Rev. James Taylor, Nov. 10, 1639.
161   "   Harriet, and Benjamin Almy, Nov. 17, 1839.
157   "   Mary Ann, and Albert G. Smith, March 11, 1840.
161   "   Emma L., and William Whitcher, Nov. 26, 1840.
155   "   Joseph, and Susan B. Albro; m. by Rev. Elijah W. Burrows, July 18, 1841.
152   "   Roxanna, and Solomon Peckham, Feb. 1, 1842.
129   "   Almira, and Capt. William Smith, Sept. 28, 1842.
130   "   Ann, and Paul M. Ennis, Nov. 15, 1842.
168   "   Joseph O., of James and Ruth, and Hannah Mary Weaver, of Benoni and Mary; m. by Rev. Joseph Smith, March 23, 1843.
157   "   Mary S., and Gideon Sprague, Nov. 20, 1844.
166   "   Hannah, and John Peckham, Dec. 25, 1845.
141   "   Eunice, and William C. Brown, Feb. 1, 1846.
164   "   Dorcas A., and George A. Carr, Jan. 16, 1848.
164   "   Lucinda W., and Joseph S. Russell, March 20, 1848.
161   "   Hiram, and Sarah P. Smith; m. by Rev. James Taylor, Oct. 1, 1848.
54   BATTEY Sarah, and Caleb B. Slocum, Feb. 6, 1800.
101   BEEBE Lydia, and Elisha Allen, Sept. 21, 1783.
63   "   Elizabeth, and Benjamin Durfee, Jr., Aug. 15, 1790.
63   "   Hannah, and Josias Wilcox, Ang. 19, 1795.
39   BILLINGTON Elisha, of South Kingstown, son of Joseph, and Abigail Brown, of Middletown, dan. of William; m. by Rev. Michael Eddy, Dec. 1, 1796.
33   BLISS William, and Barbara Phillips; m. by Rev. Nicholas Eyres, April 20, 1750.
17   "   Content, and Joseph Antunes, July 10, 1750.
109   "   Elizabeth, and Dea. William Greenman, Ang. 21, 1806.
38   BORDEN Benjamin, of Freetown, son of Benjamin and Patience, and Mary Peabody, of Joseph and Barbara, of Middletown; m. by Elisha Allen, Justice, Jan. 3, 1792.
146   "   Sarah P. and Joshua Perry, Jan. 4, 1816.
103   "   Harriet and Jonathan Coggeshall Peckham, Feb. 15, 1820.
122   BOWLER Sally, and William Peabody, Feb. 19, 1804.
100   BRIEF Elizabeth, and Charles Dyer, Jan. 21, 1716-17.
44   BROWNELL Sybel, and Soloman Sherman, May 16, 1790.
61   BROWNING Ruth, and Isaac Brown, Sept. 4, 1808.
2   BROWN Mary, and Daniel Gould, Nov. 17, 1719.
23   "   Alice, and James Phillips, Jr., March 19, 1752.
54   "   Hannah, and John Slocum, June 20, 1754.
51   "   William, and Mary Coggeshall; m. by Rev. Gardiner Thurston, May 25, 1766.
89   "   William, and Mary Coggeshall; m. by Rev. Gardiner Thurston, May 25, 1766.

89	BROWN Abigail, and Elisha Billington, Dec. 1, 1796.
125	" George, of William, and Elizabeth Peckham, of Peleg; m. by Rev. Michael Eddy, March 20, 1808.
61	" Isaac, of Gideon, of Middletown, and Ruth Browning, of George, of Portsmouth; m. by Rev. Michael Eddy, Sept. 4, 1808.
131	" Abraham, of William, of Middletown, and Lucy Little, of Nathaniel, of Little Compton; m. by Oliver H. Almy, Justice, Jan. 10, 1821.
138	" Lydia, and Rowland H. Lewis, March 26, 1838.
130	" William H., of Middletown, and Julia Ann Spooner, of Portsmouth; m. by Rev. E. W. Barrows, Nov. 24, 1842.
140	" Benjamin, of Middletown, and Emeline B. Coggeshall, of Portsmouth; m. by Rev. James Taylor, Nov. 21, 1844.
141	" William C., and Eunice Barker; m. by Rev. James Taylor, Feb. 1, 1846.
154	" Maria, and Daniel B. Smith, March 18, 1847.
169	" Mary A., and George C. Coggeshall, Dec. 19, 1849.
166	" Nathaniel A., and Sarah F. Carr; m. by Rev. S. Adlam, March 4, 1850.
168	" James A., of Savannah, Ga., and Lucy M. Brown, of Middletown; m. by Rev. S. Adlam, Aug. 20, 1855.
168	" Lucy M., and James A. Brown, Aug. 20, 1855.
43	BURGESS Sarah, and Philip Mosher, Sept. 27, 1750.
64	BURNS Walter, of Newport, and Hannah Turner, of Middletown; m. by John Barker, Justice, April 28, 1772.
18	BURROUGHS Samuel, of Newport, and Mary Greene, of Middletown; m. by Rev. Nicholas Eyres, Jan. 28, 1745-6.

C

96	CARD Elizabeth, and Holder Almy, Nov. 7, 1799.
165	CARPENTER John A., of Newport, son of William G. and Mary J. Slocum, of Gardiner T.; m. by Rev. B. Othman, Aug. 13, 1848.
164	CARR George A., and Dorcas A. Barker; m. by Rev. James Taylor, Jan. 16, 1848.
166	" Sarah F., and Nathaniel A. Brown, March 4, 1850.
61	CHAPMAN Edward, of Newport, and Ruth Bailey, of Middletown; m. by Rev. Gardiner Thurston, Nov. 7, 1765.
70	" Mrs. Ruth, and Parker Hall ; (also 74), Dec. 15, 1779.
42	CHASE Sarah, and William Earl, March 9, 1760.
101	" Zaccheus, of James, of Middletown, and James Sisson, of Preserved, of Portsmouth; m. by Rev. Michael Eddy, Aug. 14, 1814.
171	" John, and Sarah Wightman; m. at Bristol by Rev. Henry Wight, Sept. 4, 1834.
157	" James, Jr., of Middletown, and Naoma Crowsher, of Portsmouth; m. by Rev. Zalmon Tobey, Oct. 21, 1835.
156	" William, of Middletown, and Jane M. Coggeshall, of Portsmouth; m. by Rev. Elijah W. Barrows, Aug. 22, 1841.
169	" George G., of John and Susan and Hannah Mary Coggeshall, of Joshua and Deborah; m. by Rev. Joseph Smith, March 16, 1843.
149	" David B., and Sarah Peckham; m. by Rev. James Taylor, Sept. 12, 1844.
163	" William, of Middletown, and Mary C. Coggeshall, of Portsmouth; m. by Rev. James Taylor, Oct. 2, 1845.
163	" James, of John and Susan, and Sarah D. Coggeshall, of Joshua and Deborah; m. by Rev. Joseph Smith, May 6, 1847.
159	CHEESMAN James L., of New York, and Julia A. Hall, of Middletown; m. by Rev. Leland Howard, Oct. 3, 1838.
34	CHURCH Israel, of Little Compton, and Sarah Smith, of Middletown; m. by John Barker, Justice, April 10, 1757.
107	" Rachael, and Jonathan Anthony, Oct. 27, 1805.
0	CLARKE Lawrence, Jr., and Lydia Ryder, both of Newport; m. by Peleg Smith. Justice. Oct. 28, 1733.
13	" Joseph, and Elizabeth Spooner, Sept. 18, 1740.

16	CLARKE Joseph, and Phebe Negos; m. by Edward Easton, Justice, Feb. 22. 1749.	
14	CLARK Dinah, and Caleb Weeden, April 2, 1749.	
21	" Sarah, and Edward Smith, Oct. 21, 1750.	
51	" Phebe, and Samuel Thompkins, Jan. 9, 1766.	
57	" Jeremiah, of John, and Prescilla and Elizabeth Howland, of Samuel and Abigail; m. by John Sherman, Justice, at Portsmouth. Nov. 12, 1769.	
120	" Samuel, and Ruth Peckham, Dec. 9. 1773.	
72	" Walter, and Lydia Luther; m. by Rev. Gardiner Thurston, April 29, 1774.	
90	" Weston, of John, of Middletown, and Phebe Howard, of Benjamin, of Newport; m. by Rev. Michael Eddy, Feb. 12, 1800.	
120	" Samuel, and Virtue Peckham, Jan. 14, 1802.	
92	" Jedde, of George, and Mary Barker, of Matthew; m. by Rev. William Bliss. Jan. 15, 1807.	
148	" John, of Kingston, and Ruth Taggart, of Midlletown; m. at Bristol, by Rev. Isaac Lewis, Sept. 5, 1831.	
183	" Henry R., of North Kingstown, son of Benjamin T. and Mary Ann, and Rebecca Cornell, of Middletown, dan. of Samuel and Ruth; m. by Rev. Joseph Smith, March 31, 1842.	
21	COGGESHALL Thomas, of Joshua, of Newport, and Mercy Freeborn, of Gideon, of Portsmonth; m. by Benjamin Wells, Justice, March 11, 1707-8.	
28	" Comfort, and Daniel Peckham, Nov. 29, 1734.	
1	" Mary, and Joseph Nichols, Sept. 25, 1743.	
1-46	" Joshna, of Thomas, and Sarah Bailey; m. by Daniel Gould, Justice, Jan. 12, 1743-4.	
10	" Mary, and Samuel Allen, Jan. 16, 1745.	
43	" Sarah, and William Heffernan, Oct. 19, 1749.	
17	" Avis, and John Weaver, May 10, 1750.	
19	" Content, and William Weaver, Aug. 30, 1750.	
19	" Nicholas (mariner), and Sarah Phillips; m. by Daniel Gould, Justice, Dec. 6, 1750.	
22	" Rebecca, and James Weaver, Oct. 31, 1751.	
23	" Joshua, of Thomas, of Middletown, and Ann Dennis, of Joseph, of Portsmouth (also 30, 46); m. by William Anthony, Jr., Justice, Jan. 2, 1752.	
81	" Barbara, 1 Joseph Peabody, July 15, 1756.	
42	" Sarah, and Thomas Weaver, Nov. 1, 1759.	
43	" Elizabeth, and Edward Cornell, Nov. 2, 1762.	
51	" Mary, and William Brown (also 89), May 25, 1766.	
82	" Ruth, and David Wyatt, Oct. 21, 1784.	
83	" Mercy, and Thomas Manchester, April 2, 1786.	
97	" Catherine, and Alanson Peckham, Dec. 20, 1787.	
93	" Jonathan, Jr., of Jonathan, of Middletown, and Bathsheba Sherman Ward, of Joseph, dec., of Portsmouth; m. by Elder William Bliss, April 11, 1792.	
45	" John Bailey, of Thomas, of Middletown, and Mary Sanford, of Peleg, of Tiverton; m. by Elder William Bliss, Oct. 16, 1794.	
89	" Samuel, of John, of Middle own, and Nancy Peckham, of Joshua, of Portsmonth; m. by Rev. Michael Eddy, Jan. 29, 1797.	
127	" Amey Ann, and Benjamin Gardiner, Dec. 1, 1797.	
114	" Asa, of Thomas and Hester, and Sarah Barker, of Matthew and Eunice; m. by Rev. Michael Eddy, Feb. 21, 1802.	
129	" Elizabeth, and Hicks Cornell, Jan. 28, 1819.	
169	" Joseph, of Joseph and Betsey, and Lydia Cornell, of Samnel and Ruth; m. by Rev. Henry Wight, June 26, 1814.	
162	" Joshua, of Joshua, and Deborah Allen, of John; m. by Rev. Michael Eddy, Nov. 26, 1815.	
128	" David, of Anne, and Hannah Manchester, of John; m. by Joshua Coggeshall, Justice, Nov. 30, 1815.	
137	" John P., of Middletown, and Sarah Anthony, of Portsmouth; m. by Rev. Daniel Webb, Oct. 9, 1823.	
170	" Caroline C., and Daniel Weaver antumn of 1830.	

156 COGGESHALL Jane M., and William Chase, Aug. 22, 1841.
169   "   Hannah Mary, and George G. Chase, March 16, 1843.
140   "   Emeline B., and Benjamin Brown, Nov. 21, 1844.
168   "   Mary C., and William Chase, Oct. 2, 1845.
163   "   Sarah D., and James Chase, May 6, 1847.
165   "   Lydia, and Carmi Harrington, May 31, 1848.
169   "   George C., and Mary A. Brown; m. by Rev. S. Adlam, Dec. 19, 1849.
117   "   David, of Joshua and Deborah, and Sarah C. Bailey, of George L. and Mary S.; m. by Rev. John O. Charles, March 12, 1851.
168   "   Martha, and William E. Coggeshall, Aug. 12, 1855.
168   "   William E., of Middletown, and Martha Coggeshall, of Portsmouth; m. at Newport by Rev. S. Adlam, Aug. 12, 1855.
88 COOK Hannah, and John Allen, April 26, 1784.
119   "   Cynthia Ann, and William W. Peckham, Dec. 16, 1804.
12 CORNELL Thomas, of William, of Portsmouth, and Rachel Allen, of John, of Middletown; m. by William Turner, Justice, Oct. 16, 1746.
27   "   William, of Portsmouth, and Freelove Dring, of Middletown; m. by John Barker, Justice, March 27, 1754.
43   "   Edward, of Portsmouth, and Elizabeth Coggeshall, of Middletown; m. by Joseph Peabody, Justice, Nov. 2, 1762.
54   "   Robert, and Hannah Weaver; m. by John Barker, Justice, Dec. 8, 1768.
87   "   Sarah, and John Hopkins, Nov. 15, 1798.
93   "   Elizabeth, and George Peckham, Nov. 14, 1805.
169   "   Lydia, and Joseph Coggeshall, June 26, 1814.
129   "   Hicks, and Elizabeth Coggeshall; m. by Rev. Daniel Webb, Jan. 28, 1819.
133   "   Rebecca, and Henry R. Clark, March 31, 1842.
138   "   Edward M., of Tiverton, aged 23 years, son of Walter and Theresa, and Patience H. Dyer, aged 23 years, dau. of Christopher and Mary, of Portsmouth; m. by Rev. W. E. Hathaway, Aug. 5, 1849.
25 CORY Rosannah, and Clement Weaver, Sept. 9, 1744.
113 CRANDALL Elizabeth, and Samuel Stoddard, June 22, 1794.
84 CRANSTON Hannah, and Joseph Manchester, Jan. 27, 1788.
91 CROADE Elizabeth, and Gideon Barker, Oct. 25, 1781.
157 CROWSHER Naoma, and James Chase, Jr., Oct. 21, 1835.

D

85 DAVENPORT Eunice, and William Manchester, Oct. 22, 1787.
159 DAVIS Charles B., of Fall River, Mass., son of Thomas, and Mary Barker, of Mary; m. by Rev. James Taylor, Feb. 22, 1839.
110 DAWLEY Sprague, of Newport, son of George Sprague Dawley, of Exeter, and Lucy Whitman, of Paul, of Middletown; m. by Rev. Michael Eddy, March 8, 1801.
23 DENNIS Ann, and Joshua Coggeshall; (also 30, 46), Jan. 2, 1752.
95 DEVANT Phebe, and Salisbury Stoddard, June 10, 1792.
95 DEWRY Eunice, and Joseph Ryder, Jan. 7, 1813.
11 DILLINGHAM Cornelius, of Newport, and Sarah Ryder, of Middletown; m. by Edward Easton, Justice, Nov. 15, 1747.
27 DRING Freelove, and William Cornell, March 27, 1754.
70 DURFEE Phebe, and John Slocum, Jr., Oct. 2, 1777.
63   "   Benjamin, Jr., of James, and Elizabeth Beebe, of Daniel; m. by Elder William Bliss, Aug. 15, 1790.
55   "   James, of James and Ruth, of Middletown, and Mary Pearce, of South Kingstown, dau. of Timothy and Nancy; m. by Rev. William Northup, Nov. 1, 1799.
135   "   Thomas, of Middletown, and als. Elizabeth Wells, of Exeter; m. by Rev. James Taylor, July 6, 1846.
100 DYER Charles, and Elizabeth Brief; m. by Rev. Robert Billings, Jan. 21, 1716-7.

37 DYER Edward, and Abigail Stockbridge Josslyn; m. at Hanover, Mass., by
Albert Smith, Justice, Aug. 26, 1745.
37 " Charles, of Dartmouth, and Rebecca Weaver, of Middletown; m.
by John Barker, Justice, June 1, 1758.
71 " Mrs. Susannah, and Matthew Weaver, March 14, 1782.
92 " James, Jr., of James, and Hannah Allen, of Peleg; m. by Rev. William Bliss, June 7, 1792.
138 " Patience H., and Edward M. Cornell, Aug. 5, 1849.

E

42 EARL William, of Portsmouth, and Sarah Chase, of Freetown; m. by Rev.
Gardiner Thurston, March 9, 1760.
5 EASTON Mary, and John Taylor, May 10, 1744.
17 " Amey, and Samuel Gardiner, July 12, 1749.
27 " Mary, and Capt. Christopher Gardiner, Sept. 16, 1753.
35 " Hannah, and William Bailey, July 12, 1757.
46 " Mary, and Robert Lawton, June 5, 1760.
50 " Edward, and Elizabeth Turner; m. by Edward Upham, Justice,
Jan. 22, 1761.
69 " Nicholas, of Newport, and Hannah Slocum, of Matthew and Hannah, of Portsmouth; m. by Rev. Marmaduke Brown, Nov. 9,
1768.
81 " Joshua, of Newport, son of Peter, of Middletown, and Elizabeth
Slocum, of Giles, of Portsmouth; m. by Rev. Michael Eddy,
Dec. 11, 1794.
106 " Sarah, and Jonathan Hall, Nov. 15, 1795.
9 EDDY Job, of Swansey, and Patience Phillips, of James, of Middletown;
m. by Thomas Gould, Justice, Dec. 29, 1745.
82 " Ann, and Samuel Wyatt, March 12, 1775.
130 ENNIS Paul M., of South Kingstown, and Ann Barker, of Middletown, Nov.
15, 1842.

F

17 FISH Isabella, and Job Little, April 19, 1750.
19 " Mary, and John Wilson, Nov. 8, 1750.
123 " Rebecca, and Job Sherman, Oct. 24, 1805.
134 " Sally, and Isaac Manchester, Dec. 31, 1820.
11 FONES John, and Hope Sisson; m. by Edward Easton, Asst., Dec. 6, 1744.
21 FREEBORN Mercy, and Thomas Coggeshall, March 11, 1707-8.
81 " Henry, of Newport, and Nancy Peckham, of Middletown; m. by
Rev. Gardiner Thurston, July 9, 1766.

G

17 GARDINER Samuel, of Ephraim, of North Kingstown, and Amey Easton,
of Jonathan, of Middletown; m. by Daniel Coggeshall, Asst.,
July 12, 1749.
27 " Capt. Christopher, of North Kingstown, and Mrs. Mary Easton,
of Middletown; m. by Martin Howard, Justice, Sept. 16, 1753.
127 " Benjamin, of John, of South Kingstown, and Elizabeth Weeks, of
Thomas, of Warwick; m. by Rev. John Graves, Jan. 13, 1774.
127 " Benjamin, and Amey Ann Coggeshall; m. by Rev. Mr. Dehan,
Dec. 1, 1799.
127 " Benjamin, and Mary Howland, of John; m. at Jamestown, by Rev.
Mr. Dehan, March 5, 1801.
165 GIBBS Elizabeth F., and Joseph P. Weaver, Aug. 30, 1848.
160 GIFFORD Mary H., and Arnold M. Barker, Nov. 10, 1839.
2 GOULD Daniel, of Thomas and Elizabeth, of Newport, and Mary Brown, of
John, of Swansey; m. by Jonathan Nichols, Asst., Nov. 17,
1719.

65	GOULD Daniel, of Daniel, and Elizabeth Peckham, of Daniel; m. by William Stoddard, Justice, Sept. 26, 1771.
116	" Thomas, of John, and Anna Slocum, Jan. 10, 1790.
153	" Esther, and Henry Peckham, April 20, 1803.
52	" Mary, and William Smith, March 21, 1805.
116	" Henrietta, and Samuel Allen, Aug. 4, 1814.
118	" James and Sarah Weaver; m. by Rev. William Patten, Feb. 2, 1815.
119	" Sarah, and Oliver Sweet, Dec. 29, 1822.
65	GRANGER Thomas, of Newport, and Mary Larkin, of Middletown; m. by John Barker, Justice, Oct. 1, 1772.
147	GRAY Sarah Ann, and Peleg Peckham, Jr., Nov. 3, 1841.
18	GREENE Mary, and Samuel Burrows, Jan. 28, 1745-6.
18	" Sarah, and James Peckham, Jan. 28, 1745-6.
43	" Mary, and Ephraim Macomber, Jan. 11, 1750.
50	" William, and Sarah Lawton; m. by Edward Upham, Justice, Dec. 14, 1758.
101	" Sarah, and William White, Dec. 8, 1805.
109	GREENMAN Dea. William, of Stephentown, New York, son of Sylvanus, and Elizabeth Bliss, of Elder William, of Middletown; m. by Elder William Bliss, Aug. 21, 1806.

H

70-74	HALL Parker, and Ruth Chapman; m. by Rev. Gardiner Thurston, Dec. 15, 1779.
106	" Jonathan, of Newport, and Sarah Easton, of Middletown; m. by Elisha Allen, Justice, Nov. 15, 1795.
126	" J. Bailey, and Sarah Barker; m. by Rev. John B. Gibson, Nov. 22, 1810.
156	" John B., and Jenette Peckham; m. by Rev. Arthur A. Ross, Dec. 17, 1837.
159	" Julia A., and James L. Cheeseman, Oct. 3, 1838.
165	HARRINGTON Carrma, of Portsmouth, and Lydia Coggeshall; m. by Rev. James Taylor, May 31, 1848.
18	HARRIS Mercy, and Jonathan Weeden, Aug. 21, 1746.
50	HAVENS Martha, and Henry Tew, March 15, 1759.
130	HAZARD Sophia, and Peleg Peckham, Jr., July 28, 1810.
119	HEAD Rhoda, and Thomas Stoddard, Nov. 15, 1812.
43	HEFFERNAN William, of Newport, and Sarah Coggeshall, of Middletown; m. by Rev. William Vinall, Oct. 19, 1749.
6	HOAR Rebecca, and John Barker, Sept. 25, 1735.
5	" Sarah, and Robert Barker, April 20, 1738.
20	" Hezekiah, and Deborah Barker, both of Newport; m. by John Gardiner, Justice, Sept. 14, 1738.
23	" Mary, and Edward Tew, Jan. 3, 1744.
102	" Phebe, and Philip Mason, Sept. 24, 1809.
78	HOPKINS Thomas, and Phebe Woodman; m. by Rev. Gardiner Thurston, March 22, 1771.
109	" Elizabeth, and Benjamin Lake, Sept. 17, 1788.
87	" John, of Jonathan, and Sarah Cornell, of Robert; m. by Rev. Michael Eddy, Nov. 15, 1798.
90	HOWARD Phebe, and Weston Clarke, Feb. 12, 1800.
57	HOWLAND Elizabeth, and Jeremiah Clarke, Nov. 12, 1769.
80	" Benjamin Jr., of Benjamin, of East Greenwich, and Abigail Allen, of Peleg, of Middletown; m. by Rev. Michael Eddy, Dec. 22, 1799.
127	" Mary, and Benjamin Gardiner, March 5, 1801.
34	HUNT Idda, and Lott Strange, Feb 16, 1757.
117	" Susannah, and Benjam'n Allen, Feb. 11, 1808.

I

56	IRISH Mary, and Easton Bailey, March 16, 1788.
104	" Phebe, and Samuel Almy, Nov. 12, 1801.

J

34 JONES Hardin, of Newbern, N. C., and Mary Whiting, of Middletown; m. by Rev. Ezra Stiles, Oct. 17, 1756.
95 JOSLIN Olive, and William Brown Slocum, April 28, 1793.
37 JOSSELYN Abigail Stockbridge, and Edward Dyer, Aug. 26, 1845.

K

73 KEMPTON Rebecca, and Levi Barker, May 12, 1793.

L

109 LAKE Benjamin, and Elizabeth Hopkins; m. by Joseph Peabody, Justice, Sept. 17, 1788.
65 LARKIN Mary, and Thomas Granger, Oct. 1, 1772.
50 LAWTON Sarah, and William Greene, Dec. 14, 1758.
46 " Robert, of Newport, and Mary Easton, of Middletown; m. by John Gardiner, Dep. Governor, June 5, 1760.
123 " Sarah, and Peckham Anthony, Oct. 1, 1801.
128 " Mary Ann, and John N. Northup, June 16, 1844.
188 LEWIS Rowland H., of New Shoreham, and Lydia Brown, of Abraham, of Middletown; m. by Rev. James Taylor, March 26, 1888.
17 LITTLE Job, and Isabella Fish; m. by Daniel Gould, Justice, April 19, 1750.
79 " Lucy, and William Allen, Aug. 12, 1761.
131 " Lucy, and Abraham Brown, Jan. 10, 1821.
72 LUTHER Lydia, and Walter Clarke, April 20, 1774.

M

43 MACUMBER Ephraim, of Newport, and Mary Greene, of Middletown; m. by Rev. William Vinall, Jan. 11, 1750.
72 " Mary, and Clarke Taggart, June 5, 1783.
90 " Elizabeth, and William Taggart, Feb. 6, 1791.
97 " John, of Jeremiah, dec., of Middletown, and Ruth Taber, of Samuel, of Tiverton; m. by Rev. Peleg Burrough, 3m., 23d, 1794.
75 MANCHESTER Isaac, Jr., of Middletown, and Phebe Taylor, of Reuben, of Portsmouth; m. by Elder William Bliss, Sept. 4, 1785.
93 " Thomas, of Isaac, and Mercy Coggesball, of Joshua; m. by Rev. William Bliss, April 2, 1786.
84 " John, of Isaac, and Sarah Wood, of John; m. by Elder William Bliss, Mar. 8, 1787.
85 " William, of Isaac, of Middletown, and Eunice Davenport, of Jonathan, of Portsmouth; m. by Elder William Bliss, Oct. 29, 1787.
84 " Joseph, of Isaac, and Hannah Cranston, of Richmond; m. by Elder William Bliss, Jan. 27, 1788.
118 " Lydia, and Parker Weaver, Sept. 7, 1809.
128 " Hannah, and David Coggeshall, Nov. 30, 1815.
128 " Mary, and Phillip Anthony, Dec. 4, 1817.
113 " Freeborn, of Thomas, of Middletown, and Ann Slocum, of Stephen, of Portsmouth; m. by Rev. Michael Eddy, July 2, 1818.
134 " Isaac, of Thomas, of Middletown, and Sally Fish, of John, of Portsmouth; m. by Thomas Cory, Jr., Justice, Dec. 31, 1820.
148 " Mercy, and Benjamin Peckham, July 5, 1831.
38 MARTIN George, and Barbara —— ; m. by James Clarke, Justice, Mar. 28, 1739.
58 MASON Rhoda, and James Barker, 3d, Aug. 16, 1770.
133 MAXON Wealthy Ann, and John B. Wood, Dec. 25, 1822.

109   MICHELL Peter, of Richard, of Middletown, and Mary Wales, of Peter, of
           Portsmouth : m. by Rev. Michael Eddy, Aug. 21, 1806.
 48   MOSHIER Philip, and Sarah Burgess ; m. by Rev. William Vinall, Sept. 27,
           1750.

N

102   NASON Philip, of Adams, Mass., and Phebe Hoar, of Middletown ; m. by
           Rev. John B. Gibson, Sept. 24, 1809.
 16   NEGAS Phebe, and Joseph Clarke, Feb. 22, 1749.
  1   NICHOLS Joseph, and Mary Coggeshall, of John ; m. by Daniel Gould, Justice,
           Sept. 25, 1743.
128   NORTHRUP John N., of Middletown, and Mary Ann Lawton, of Ports-
           mouth ; m. by Rev. James Taylor, June 16, 1844.

O P

158   PALMER Henry E., and Sarah S. Peckham ; m. by Rev. E. W. Barrows,
           March 6, 1842.
 16   PEABODY John, and Dorcas Sweet, both of Newport ; m. by Peleg Smith,
           Justice, Jan. 5, 1734-5.
 14   "   Rachel, and Henry Smith, April 26, 1841.
 81   "   Joseph, and Barbara Coggeshall ; m. by John Taylor, Justice, July
                  15, 1756.
 88   "   Mary, and Benjamin Borden, Jan. 3, 1792.
122   "   William, of Middletown, and Solly Bowler, of Hopkinton ; m. at
                  Hopkinton, by Elder Abram Coon. Feb. 19, 1804.
143   "   Easton, and Mary Slocum ; m. by Rev. Michael Eddy, Dec. 22,
                  1816.
 55   "   Mary, and James Durfee, Nov. 1, 1799.
 28   PECKHAM Daniel, of Joseph, and Comfort Coggeshall, o' Thomas, both of
           Newport ; m. by Job Lawton, Justice, Nov. 29, 1734.
 41   "   Sarah, and William Weeden, May 12, 1739.
 18   "   James, and Sarah Greene ; m. by Rev. Nicholas Eyres, Jan. 28,
                  1745-6.
 14   "   Ann, and James Barker (also 43), Jan. 5, 1748.
 50   "   Sarah, and William Peckham, 3d, Oct. 5, 1758.
 50   "   William, 3d, and Sarah Peckham ; m. by Edward Upham, Justice,
                  Oct. 5, 1758.
 50   "   William, and Lydia Rogers ; m. by Edward Upham, Justice, March
                  20, 1760.
 50   "   Joseph, and Sarah Weeden ; m. by Edward Upham, Justice, Nov.
                  20, 1760.
 51   "   Nancy, and Henry Freeborn, July 9, 1766.
 53   "   Phebe, and Elisha Barker, Nov. 8, 1767.
 65   "   Elizabeth, and Daniel Gould, Sept. 26, 1771.
 66   "   Peleg, and Elizabeth Smith ; m. by Rev. Gardiner Thurston, Oct.
                  25, 1772.
120   "   Ruth, and Samuel Clarke, Dec. 9, 1773.
 71   "   Sarah, and Isaac Barker, Dec. 2, 1775.
 73   "   Thomas, and Hannah Weaver ; m. at South Kingstown, June 29,
                  1778.
 66   "   Levi, of Samuel, dec., of Middletown, and Sarah Tripp of Samuel,
                  of East Greenwich ; m. at East Greenwich by Elder John Gor-
                  ton, Sept. 24, 1760.
 59   "   Samuel, of Samuel and Mrs. Elizabeth Weaver, of William ; m. by
                  Oliver Durfee, Justice, Dec. 20, 1781.
105   "   Isaac, of Joseph and Sarah, of Middletown, and Ruth Tripp of Sam-
                  uel and Catherine, of East Greenwich ; m. at East Greenwich
                  by Elder John Gorton, Dec. 9, 1785.
 97   "   Alanson, of Joseph and Sarah and Catherine Coggeshall, of Jona-
                  than and Sarah ; m. by Elder William Bliss, Dec. 20, 1787.
 89   "   Nancy, and Samuel Coggeshall, Jan. 29, 1797.

124   PECKHAM Benjamin, of Sarah, and Sarah Peckham, of Joshua; m. by Rev.
          Michael Eddy, Jan. 1, 1800.
124   "   Sarah, and Benjamin Peckham, Jan. 1, 1800.
74   "   Samuel, of Levi, of Middletown, and Sarah Phillips, of Joseph, of
          Newport; m. by Rev. Michael Eddy, Nov. 27, 1801.
120   "   Virtue, and Samuel Clarke, Jan. 14, 1802.
41   "   Russell G., of Lewis, of Middletown, and Louisa Sisson, of Richard,
          of Portsmouth; m. by Rev. Michael Eddy, at Newport, March 3,
          1803.
153   "   Henry, of Peleg and Esther Gould, of Middletown, dau. of Nicholas
          of South Kingstown; m. by Rev. Michael Eddy, April 20, 1803.
111   "   Mary, and Nathaniel Barker, Dec. 1, 1803.
119   "   William W., of Samuel, of Middletown, and Cynthia Ann Cook, of
          Job, of Portsmouth; m. by Rev. Michael Eddy, Dec. 16, 1804.
93   "   George, of Josephus, of South Kingstown, and Elizabeth Cornell, of
          Robert, of Middletown; m. by Rev. Michael Eddy, Nov. 14,
          1805.
121   "   Gideon and Cynthia Barker; m. by Joshua Bradley, Jan. 2,
          1806.
85   "   Daniel, of Richard, and Catherine Barker, of Peleg; m. by Rev.
          Michael Eddy, Nov. 2, 1806.
125   "   Elizabeth, and George Brown, March 20, 1808.
130   "   Peleg, Jr., of Peleg, and Sophia Hazard, of George, dec.; m. by
          Thomas Cory, Jr., Justice, July 28, 1810.
86   "   Esther, and Joseph Barker, Jan. 16, 1814.
112   "   Elisha, of Peleg, of Middletown, and Elizabeth D. Sylvester, of
          Newport, dau. of John; m. by Rev. Michael Eddy, Feb. 16,
          1815.
60   "   Mary, and Benoni Weaver, Dec. 12, 1815.
144   "   William, of John, and Anne Smith, of Edward; m. by Rev. Michael
          Eddy, Feb. 20, 1818.
103   "   Jonathan Coggeshall, and Harriet Borden; m. by Rev. Michael
          Eddy, Feb. 15, 1820.
153   "   Henry, of Henry; m. Nov. 28, 1826.
153   "   Lydia B., of Henry; m. Jan. 17, 1827.
139   "   Sarah, and William Smith, May 24, 1827.
152   "   Restcome, of Middletown, and Ruth Sherman, of Portsmouth,
          Dec. 6, 1827.
137   "   William Smith, Jr., and Ruth Ann Wyatt; m. by Rev. Michael
          Eddy, March 23, 1828.
153   "   Abby Ardelia, of Henry; m. June 20, 1829.
147   "   John C., of Gideon, and Barbara Ryder, of William, dec.; m. by
          Rev. Henry Sullings, April 14, 1831.
148   "   Benjamin, of Middletown, and Mercy Manchester, of Westport,
          Mass.; m. by Rev. Henry Sullings, July 5, 1831.
151   "   Wealthy, and Isaac Barker, June 23, 1833.
156   "   Jenette, and John B. Hall, Dec. 17, 1837.
147   "   Peleg, Jr., of Middletown, and Sarah Ann Gray, of Tiverton; m. by
          Rev. E. W. Barrows, Nov. 3, 1841.
152   "   Solomon, of Newport, and Roxanna Barker, of Middletown; m.
          by Rev. E. W. Barrows, Feb. 1, 1842.
158   "   Sarah S., and Henry E. Palmer, March 6, 1842.
149   "   Sarah, and David B. Chase, Sept. 12, 1844.
166   "   John, and Hannah Barker; m. by Rev. W. W. Evert, Dec. 25, 1845.
159   "   Abbie Frances, and George B. Weaver, Dec. 16, 1847.
146   PERRY Joshua, of Joseph, of Newport, and Sarah P. Borden, of Benja-
          min, of Middletown; m. by Rev. Michael Eddy, Jan. 4, 1816.
136   "   Patience, and Charles Anthony, Feb. 17, 1828.
0   PHILLIPS Patience, and Job Eddy, Dec. 29, 1745.
33   "   Barbara, and William Bliss, April 20, 1750.
19   "   Sarah, and Nicholas Coggeshall, Dec. 6, 1750.
23   "   James, Jr., and Alice Brown, of Nicholas; m. by Daniel Gould,
          Justice, March 19, 1752.
74   "   Sarah, and Samuel Peckham, Nov. 27, 1801.
52   PITMAN Moses, of Newport, and Phebe Weeden, of Middletown; m. by Wil-
          liam Bailey, Justice, Feb. 3, 1767.

Q R

52	RICE James, and Isabel Sherman; m. by William Bailey, Justice, Oct. 16, 1766.
84	ROBERTSON Mary, and Benjamin Barker, Feb. 18, 1789.
50	ROGERS Lydia, and William Peckham, March 20, 1760.
164	RUSSELL Joseph S., formerly of Dartmouth, aged 42 years, son of Joseph and Marian, and Lucinda W. Barker, of Portsmouth, aged 20 years, dau. of Susan and David; intention published March 16, 1848, by the Rev. James Taylor, at Middletown; m. March 20, 1848.
6	RYDER Lydia, and Lawrence Clarke, Jr., Oct. 28, 1733.
11	" Sarah, and Cornelius Dillingham, Nov. 15, 1747.
61	" Mary, and Samuel Bailey, June 7, 1769.
76	" William, and Abigail Wood; m. by Rev. Gardiner Thurston, Jan. 29, 1784.
95	" Joseph, and Eunice Dewey; m. by Elder Asher Miner, Jan. 7, 1813.
121	" Mrs. Jane, and David Wyatt, Oct. 22, 1820.
147	" Barbara, and John C. Peckham, April 14, 1831.

S

24	SANFORD Frances, and Robert Barker, Feb. 15, 1753.
36	" Giles, of Dartmouth, and Elizabeth Smith, of Middletown; m. by John Barker, Justice, March 12, 1758.
45	" Mary, and John Bailey Coggeshall, Oct. 16, 1794.
112	" Lillas, and Giles Barker, Oct. 23, 1803.
112	" Lydia, and Elizabeth Barker, Feb. 16, 1816.
149	" Lavina, and Henry Taber, 12m. 4th, 1831.
5	SEAGER Judith, and John Taylor, Oct. 3, 1717.
98	SHAW Mary, and John Wood, Dec. —, 1744.
104	SHEFFIELD Benjamin T., of South Kingstown, son of Nathan and Mary Barker, of Elisha, of Middletown; m. by Rev. Michael Eddy, Dec. 10, 1801.
15	SHELDON Jonathan, of Providence, and Mary Taylor, of John, of Middletown; m. by Daniel Gould, Justice, Sept. 21, 1749.
55	" Sarah, and Rowland Allen, Dec. 28, 1769.
35	SHERMAN Thomas, Jr., of Portsmouth, and Idda Tripp, of Middletown; m. by John Barker, Justice, Oct. 6, 1757.
52	" Isabel, and James Rice, Oct. 16, 1766.
68	" Mrs. Eunice, and David Barker, Oct. 1, 1772.
44	" Solomon, of Middletown, son of Benoni, of North Kingstown, and Sybel Brownell, of Middletown, dau. of Timothy, of North Plains, Mass.; m. by Elder William Bliss, May 16, 1790.
122	" Job, of Preserved and Rebecca Fish, of Robert, both of Portsmouth; m. by Rev. Michael Eddy, Oct. 24, 1805.
145	" Eliza, and Gardiner Thurston Slocum, Sept. 23, 1824.
152	" Ruth, and Restcome Peckham, Dec. 6, 1827.
167	" Julia M., and Job M. Barker, May 3, 1837.
1	SHRIEVES Thomas, of Portsmouth, and Ruth Weaver, of Middletown; m. by Daniel Gould, Justice, Jan. 12, 1743-4.
11	SISSON Hope, and John Fones, Dec. 6, 1747.
69	" Phebe, and David Albro, Oct. 13, 1796.
41	" Louisa, and Russell G. Peckham, March 3, 1803.
101	" Jane, and Zaccheas Chase, Aug. 14, 1814.
126	" Robert C., and Rhoda Anthony; m. by Rev. Michael Eddy, Sept. 5, 1824.
4	SLOCUM Mary, and William Barker, Jr., Nov. 5, 1744.
29	" Mary, and William Tucker, July 18, 1755.
54	" John, and Hannah Brown; m. by John Gardiner, Dep. Governor, June 20, 1754.
50	" Avis, and Reuben Taylor, Feb. 12, 1761.
69	" Hannah, and Nicholas Easton, Nov. 9, 1768.

70	SLOCUM	John, Jr., and Phebe Durfee; m. by Rev. Erasmus Kelley, Oct. 2, 1777.
145	"	William, and Mrs. Mary Bailey; m. by Rev. Gardiner Thurston, May 30, 1785.
116	"	Anna, and Thomas Gould, Jan. 10, 1790.
54	"	Joseph Wanton, of Middletown, son of John, of North Kingstown, and Rhoda Stoddard, of Salisbury, of Middletown; m. by Rev. Michael Eddy, Aug. 7, 1791.
95	"	William Brown, of John, of Middletown, and Olive Joslin, of Stockbridge, of Pembroke, Mass.; m. by Elder William Bliss, April 28, 1793.
81	"	Elizabeth, and Joshua Easton, Dec. 14, 1794.
54	"	Caleb B., of Portsmouth, son of John and Sarah Battey, of Jamestown, dan. of John; m. by Rev. Michael Eddy, Feb. 6, 1800.
111	"	Sarah, and Christopher Vars, Jan. 19, 1809.
143	"	Mary, and Easton Peabody, Dec. 22, 1816.
113	"	Ann, and Freeborn Manchester, July 2, 1818.
145	"	Gardiner Thurston, of Middletown, and Eliza Sherman, of Portsmouth; m. by Rev. William Gammell, Sept. 23, 1824.
158	"	Rhoda, and James Wyatt, March 13, 1842.
136	"	Mary Ann, and Benjamin Wyatt, Feb. 6, 1843.
165	"	Mary J., and John A. Carpenter, Aug. 13, 1848.
2	SMITH	Phebe, and Robert Barker, Oct. 25, 1733.
14	"	Henry, and Rachel Peabody, April 26, 1741.
21	"	Edward, of Middletown, and Sarah Clarke, of Newport; m. by Rev. William Vinall, Oct. 21, 1750.
34	"	Sarah, and Israel Church, April 10, 1757.
36	"	Elizabeth, and Giles Sanford, March 12, 1758.
66	"	Elizabeth, and Peleg Peckham, Oct. 25, 1772.
96	"	Sarah, and Samuel Barker, April 26, 1781.
100	"	George, and Rebecca Barker; m. by Rev. Gardiner Thurston, Nov. 23, 1796.
52	"	William, of Middletown, and Mary Gould, of South Kingstown; m. by Samuel Helme, Justice, March 21, 1805.
144	"	Anne, and William Peckham, Feb. 20, 1818.
141	"	Sarah Anne, and William Taggart, Dec. 12, 1822.
129	"	William, and Sarah Peckham; m. by Rev. Michael Eddy, May 24, 1827.
157	"	Albert G., and Mary Ann Barker; m. by Rev. Leland Howard, March 11, 1840.
129	"	Capt. William, of George and Rebecca, and Almira Barker, of Stephen and Martha; m. by Rev. Joseph Smith, Sept. 28, 1842.
154	"	Daniel B., and Maria Brown; m. by Rev. James Taylor, March 18, 1847.
161	"	Sarah P., and Hiram Barker, Oct. 1, 1848.
13	SPOONER	Elizabeth, and Joseph Clarke, Sept. 18, 1740.
130	"	Julia Ann, and William H. Brown, Nov. 24, 1842.
157	SPRAGUE	Gideon, of New Shoreham, and Mary S. Barker, of Middletown; m. by Rev. Thomas Leaver, Nov. 20, 1844.
54	STODDARD	Rhoda, and Joseph Wanton Slocum, Aug. 7, 1791.
95	"	Salisbury, and Phebe Devant; m. by William Borden, Justice, June 10, 1792.
113	"	Samuel, of Salisbury, of Middletown, and Elizabeth Crandall, of Thomas; m. by Rev. Michael Eddy, June 22, 1794.
119	"	Thomas, of Salisbury, dec., and Phebe, of Middletown, and Rhoda Head, of Lovet and Mary, of Little Compton; m. at Little Compton by Rev. Mase Shepard, Nov. 15, 1812.
34	STRANGE	Lott, and Idda Hunt; m. by John Barker, Justice, Feb. 16, 1757.
150	SULLINGS	William P., of New Bedford, trader, aged 36 years, widower, and Martha A. Barker, of New Bedford, aged 28 years, dau of Stephen and Martha, intention Jan. 1, 1847; m. by Rev. James Taylor at Middletown, Jan. 1, 1847.

16 SWEET Dorcas, and John Peabody, Jan. 5, 1734-35.
75   "   George, of Samuel of North Kingstown, and Mary Whitman, of
            Paul, of Middletown; m. by Rev. Michael Eddy, Jan. 31, 1802.
119   "   Oliver, and Sarah Gould; m. by Rev. Michael Eddy, Dec. 29,
            1822.
112 SYLVESTER Elizabeth D., and Elisha Peckham, Feb. 16, 1815.

T

17 TABER Ruth, and John Macumber, 3m. 23d., 1794.
133   "   George, and Sarah P. Taggart; m. by Rev. Michael Eddy, Aug. 18,
            1825.
149   "   Henry, and Lavina Sanford; m. by Rev. James A. McKensie, at
            Newport, 12m. 4d., 1831.
72 TAGGART Clarke, and Mary Macumber; m. by Joseph Peabody, Justice,
            June 5, 1783.
90   "   William, and Elizabeth Macumber; m. by Joseph Peabody, Jus-
            tice, Feb. 6, 1791.
141   "   William, of Joseph and Sarah Anne Smith, of Jamestown; m. by
            Rev. Michael Eddy, Dec. 12, 1822.
133   "   Sarah P., and George Taber, Aug. 18, 1825.
148   "   Ruth, and John Clarke, Sept. 5, 1831.
5   TAYLOR John, of Newport, and Judith Seager, of Kings Towne; m. by
            Rouse Helme, Asst., Oct. 3, 1717.
5   "   John, and Mary Easton, both of Newport; m. by Peleg Smith, May
            10, 1744.
15   "   Mary, and Jonathan Sheldon, Sept. 21, 1749.
50   "   Reuben, and Avis Slocum; m. by Edward Upham, Justice, Feb. 12,
            1761.
75   "   Phebe, and Isaac Manchester, Jr., Sept. 4, 1785.
151   "   Mary, and John C. Barker, March 1, 1832.
23 TEW Edward, and Mary Hoar; m at Dighton, Mass., by Rev. Nathaniel
            Fisher, Jan. 3, 1744.
35   "   Henry, of Jamestown, and Desire Tripp, of Middletown; m. by
            John Barker, Justice, Sept. 18, 1757.
50   "   Henry, and Martha Havens; m. by Edward Upham, Justice, March
            15, 1759.
42   "   Mary, and Giles Barker, April 13, 1760.
51 THOMPKINS Samuel, of Newport, and Phebe Clarke, of Middletown; m.
            by Rev. Gardiner Thurston, Jan. 9, 1766.
42 TOMPKINS Sarah, and Samuel Tripp, June 15, 1760.
64 TORREY Josiah, of Middletown, Conn., and Susanna Turner, of Middletown,
            R. I.; m. by Rev. Ezra Stiles, Oct. 31, 1771.
35 TRIPP Desire, and Henry Tew, Sept. 18, 1757.
35   "   Idda, and Thomas Sherman, Jr., Oct. 6, 1757.
42   "   Samuel, of Portsmouth, and Sarah Tompkins, of Middletown; m. by
            Rev. Gardiner Thurston, June 15, 1760.
66   "   Sarah, and Levi Peckham, Sept. 24, 1780.
105   "   Ruth, and Isaac Peckham, Dec. 9, 1785.
29 TUCKER William, and Mary Slocum, both of Dartmouth; m. by John Bar-
            ker, Justice, July 18, 1755.
50 TURNER Elizabeth, and Edward Easton, Jan. 22, 1761.
64   "   Susanna, and Josiah Torrey, Oct. 31, 1771.
64   "   Hannah, and Walter Burns, April 28, 1772.

U V

111 VARS Christopher, and Sarah Slocum; m. by Rev. John B. Gibson, Jan.
            19, 1809.
18 VICKERY Mary, and Jonathan Weeden, Nov. 30, 1749.

W

109	WALES Mary, and Peter Mitchell, Aug. 21, 1806.
76	WARD Abigail, and William Ryder, Jan. 29, 1784.
115	" Mary, and Peleg Barker, June 3, 1784.
93	" Bathsheba Sherman, and Jonathan Coggeshall, Jr., April 11, 1792.
106	" John, of Portsmonth, son of Joseph, and Sarah Wyatt, of Samuel, of Middletown; m. by Elisha Allen, Justice, July 15, 1798.
133	" John B., and Wealthy Ann Maxson; m. by Rev. Michael Eddy, Dec. 25, 1822.
168	" Gilbert L and Sarah Weaver; m. by Rev. James Taylor, Jan. 14, 1849.
1	WEAVER Ruth, and Thomas Shrieves, Jan. 12, 1743-4.
25	" Clement, Jr., of Middletown, and Rosannah Cory, of Tiverton; m. by Job Almy, Justice, (also 28), Sept. 9, 1744.
14	" Mary, and Thomas Weaver, Feb. 16, 1748.
14	" Thomas, of Thomas, Jr., and Mary Weaver, of Benjamin; m. by Daniel Gould, Justice, Feb. 16, 1748.
17	" John, of West Greenwich, and Avis Coggeshall, of Middletown; m. by Daniel Gould, Justice, May 10, 1750.
19	" William, and Content Coggeshall; m. by Daniel Gould, Justice, Aug. 30, 1750.
22	" James, and Rebecca Coggeshall; m. by Daniel Gould, Justice, Oct. 31, 1751.
30	" Alice, and Thomas Weaver, Jan. 1, 1756.
30	" Thomas, of Middletown, and Alice Weaver, of Portsmonth; m. by Robert Lawton, Asst., Jan. 1, 1756.
37	" Rebecca, and Charles Dyer, June 1, 1758.
42	" Thomas, and Sarah Coggeshall; m. by John Taylor, Justice, Nov. 1, 1759.
54	" Hannah, and Robert Cornell, Dec. 8, 1768.
73	" Hannah, and Thomas Peckham, June 29, 1778.
59	" Elizabeth, and Samuel Peckham, Dec. 20, 1781.
71	" Matthew, and Mrs. Susannah Dyer; m. by Oliver Durfee, Justice, March 14, 1782.
118	" Parker, of Matthew, and Lydia Manchester, of Thomas; m. by Rev. Michael Eddy, Sept. 7, 1809.
118	" Sarah, and James Gould, Feb. 2, 1815.
60	" Benont, of Hannah, and Mary Peckham, of Levi; m. by Rev. Michael Eddy, Dec. 12, 1815.
170	" Daniel, and Caroline C. Coggeshall, of Jonathan and Bathsheba, autumn of 1830.
168	" Hannah Mary, and Joseph O. Barker, March 23, 1843.
159	" George B., and Abba Frances Peckham; m. by Rev. Hobart Williams, Dec. 16, 1847.
165	" Joseph P., of Benoni and Mary, of Middletown, and Elizabeth T. Gibbs, of Portsmouth, dan. of Enos and Sarah; m. by Rev. Joseph Smith, Aug. 30, 1848.
166	" Sarah, and Gilbert L. Ward, Jan. 14, 1849.
41	WEEDEN William, and Sarah Peckham, of Isaac; m. by Rev. John Callender, Jr., May 12, 1739.
18	" Jonathan, of Newport, and Mercy Harris, of Middletown; m. by Rev. Nicholas Eyres, Aug. 21, 1746.
14	" Caleb, and Dinah Clarke, widow; m. by Daniel Gould, Justice, April 2, 1749.
18	" Jonathan, and Mary Vickers; m. by Rev. Nicholas Eyres, Nov. 30, 1744.
50	" Sarah, and Joseph Peckham, Nov. 20, 1760.
52	" Phebe, and Moses Pitman, Feb. 3, 1767.
127	WEEKES Elizabeth, and Benjamin Gardiner, Jan. 13, 1774.
36	WELLES Gideon, of Weathersfield, Conn., and Wealthian Whiting, of Middletown; m. by Rev. Ezra Stiles, Nov. 24, 1757.
135	WELLS Mrs. Elizabeth, and Thomas Durfee, July 6, 1846.
161	WHITCHER William, of Springfield, Mass., and Emma L. Borden, of Providence; m. by Rev. E. W. Barrows, Nov. 26, 1840.

101	WHITE William (blacksmith), and Sarah Greene, widow of Benjamin, both of Newport; m. by Elisha Allen, Justice, Dec. 8, 1805.
34	WHITING Mary, and Hardin Jones, Oct. 17, 1756.
36	" Wealthian, and Gideon Welles, Nov. 24, 1757.
110	WHITMAN Lucy, and Sprague Dawfey, Mar. 8, 1801.
75	" Mary, and George Sweet, Jan. 31, 1802.
11	WILBOUR Sarah, and Gershom Wood, Nov. 8, 1747.
68	WILCOX Josias, and Hanna Beebe; m. by Oliver Durfee, Justice, Aug. 19, 1795.
140	" Ruth, and James Barker, May 5, 1814.
171	WIGHTMAN Sarah, and John Chase, Sept. 4, 1834.
19	WILSON John, of Jamestown, and Mary Fish, of Middletown; m. by Daniel Gould Justice, Nov. 8, 1750.
78	WOODMAN Phebe, and Thomas Hopkins, Mar. 22, 1771.
98	WOOD John, of Middletown, and Mary, Shaw, of Little Compton; m. at Little Compton, by Rev. Robert Billings, Dec. —, 1744.
11	" Gershom, and Sarah Wilbour, widow: m. by Thomas Gould, Justice, Nov. 8, 1747.
84	" Sarah, and John Manchester, Mar. 8, 1787.
82	WYATT Samuel, and Ann Eddy; m. by Rev. Erasmus Kelly, Mar. 12, 1775.
82	" David, of Samuel, and Ruth Coggeshall, of Thomas; m. by Rev. Michael Eddy, Oct. 21, 1784.
106	" Sarah, and John Ward, July 15, 1778.
121	" David, and Mrs. Jane Ryder; m. by Rev. Daniel Webb, Oct. 22, 1820.
132	" Thomas C., and Silvester Anthony; m. by Rev. Michael Eddy, Mar. 13, 1825.
137	" Ruth Ann, and William Smith Peckham, Mar. 23, 1828.
158	" Bathana C., and William C. Allen, Dec. 29, 1836.
160	" William T., of Nathaniel, and Ann Barker, of Sarah; m. by Rev. James Taylor, Mar. 31, 1839.
158	" James, of Middletown, and Rhoda Slocum, of Portsmouth; m. by Rev. E. W. Barrows, Mar. 13, 1842.
136	" Benjamin, and Mary Ann Slocum; m. by Rev. E. W. Barrows, Feb. 6, 1843.

Note.—Nothing recorded under letters   X   Y   Z.

MIDDLETOWN.

BIRTHS AND DEATHS.

A

69	ALBRO	Alice, of David, Jr., and Phebe,	Aug. 7, 1797.
69	"	Peleg,	Dec. 6, 1797.
69	"	Lydia,	Nov. 26, 1802.
91	"	Mehitable,	April 26, 1804.
91	"	Edmund,	April 16, 1806.
91	"	Stephen,	May 5, 1809.
91	"	Freeborn,	Oct. 20, 1811.
91	"	Arnold,	Jan. 31, 1814.
42	ALLEN	John, Dec. 27, 1691,	d. Nov. 6, 1733.
65	"	Peleg, of John and Elizabeth,	March 21, 1734.
10	"	Rowland, of Samuel and Mary,	Oct. 15, 1746.
19	"	Noel,	March 26, 1749.
23	"	Joseph,	Feb. 4, 1752.
28	"	John,	Dec. 2, 1753.
42	"	Thomas,	Sept. 9, 1759.
77	"	Mary, wife of Samuel,	d. March 17, 1768.
80	"	Hannah, of Peleg and Elizabeth,	Oct. 16, 1765.
80	"	Elizabeth,	Feb. 27, 1768.
80	"	Susannah,	March 11, 1770.
80	"	Abigail,	Aug. 1, 1772.
80	"	Martha,	July 22, 1775.
80	"	Rachel,	March 20, 1778.
80	"	Anne,	March 4, 1781.
80	"	Phebe,	April 3, 1783.
81	"	Noel, of Joseph and Mary,	May 12, 1780.
81	"	Samuel,	Nov. 4, 1781.
81	"	Thomas,	July 25, 1783.
81	"	Mary,	June 6, 1785.
79	"	Ruth, of William and Lucy,	Nov. 2, 1781.
79	"	Clarrissa,	June 6, 1784.
79	"	Nancy,	Aug. 11, 1787.
79	"	Selma,	Jan. 9, 1790.
79	"	George,	Sept. 22, 1792.
79	"	William,	May 15, 1794.
79	"	Mary,	June 4, 1797.
79	"	Hannah,	April 11, 1799.
79	"	Peleg,	April 6, 1803.
79	"	Thomas Cornell,	Sept. 29, 1807.
101	"	Benjamin, of Elisha and Lydia,	Feb. 13, 1784.
101	"	Robert Taylor Stanton,	July 17, 1785.
88	"	Deborah, of John and Hannah,	July 7, 1784.
88	"	Thank'ul,	Nov. 27, 1785.
88	"	Samuel,	July 28, 1787.
175	"	Hannah, wife of John,	d. July 15, 1788.
175	"	Peleg, died in 67th year,	Feb. 10, 1801.
117	"	Elizabeth, of Benjamin and Susannah,	Jan. 11, 1809.
117	"	Amey,	Jan. 16, 1811.
117	"	Lydia Stanton,	April 18, 1813.
117	"	Ruth,	Feb. 12, 1815.

117	ALLEN	Robert Taylor Stanton, of Benjamin and Susannah,	June 19, 1820.
117	"	Benjamin,	May 14, 1822.
117	"	Sarah,	March 8, 1825.
174	"	Lydia, wife of Elisha,	d. Feb. 6, 1815.
174	"	Ruth, of John and Elizabeth,	d. July 9, 1820.
174	"	Elisha, died in his 92d year, had been Town Clerk o' Middletown nearly 46 years,	April 10, 1829.
107	ANTHONY	Jonathan, of Gould and Abigail,	12m. 26th, 1785.
103	"	Elam, of Jonathan and Lydia,	10m., 5th, 1790.
103	"	Jacob,	3m., 20th, 1792.
103	"	Asa,	2m., 12th, 1794.
103	"	Ruth,	1m., 26th, 1796.
103	"	Silas,	4m., 25th, 1798.
103 .	"	Josiah,	8m., 28th, 1800.
90	"	Jacob Gould, of Gould and Bathsheba	3m., 6th, 1799.
123	"	Rhoda, of Peckham and Sarah,	June 26, 1802.
123	"	Charles,	Sept. 12, 1803.
123	"	Sylvester,	Sept. 16, 1805.
123	"	Mary Ann,	May 31, 1809.
123	"	Sarah,	Oct. 12, 1812.
123	"	Hannah,	Dec. 17, 1814.
123	"	George Peckham,	Dec. 15, 1821.
123	"	Sarah Anne, dau. of above Hannah,	Jan. 3, 1833.
155	"	Gideon,	Sept. 19, 1819.
155	"	Sarah W.,	Feb. 9, 1821.
155	"	John M.,	Aug. 31, 1823.
155	"	Elizabeth C.,	Sept. 1, 1825.
155	"	Susan Ann,	Oct. 7, 1828.
26	ANTUNES	Elizabeth, of Joseph and Content,	April 26, 1751.
26	"	Joseph,	Oct. 26, 1752.

B

32	BAILEY	Sarah, of Samuel and Alice,	Feb. 14, 1727.
32	"	Sarah,	d. Nov. 4, 1750.
32	"	William,	Jan. 24, 1730.
32	"	John,	June 7, 1733.
32	"	Samuel,	Feb. 20, 1734.
32	"	Ruth,	May 24, 1739.
26	"	Mary, of James and Abigail,	April 6, 1752.
90	"	Robert,	July 6, 1763.
29	"	Jemima,	Oct. 17, 1754.
45	"	Jonathan, of William and Hannah,	Sept. 7, 1759.
56	"	Easton,	Sept. 29, 1764.
66	"	Sarah,	Feb. 7, 1766.
56	"	William,	Aug. 26, 1768.
61	"	John, of Samuel and Mary,	Sept. 10, 1771.
56	"	John, of Easton and Mary,	July 12, 1789.
56	"	Patience,	Jan. 21, 1791.
56	"	William,	Sept. 1, 1792.
56	"	Patience, 2d,	May 10, 1794.
56	"	George Irish,	April 7, 1797.
56	"	Isaac,	June 22, 1799.
92	"	Hannah, of William and Sarah,	Sept. 9, 1799.
49	"	John, of William, 2d, and Lydia,	May 14, 1815.
49	"	Mary Irish,	Feb. 27, 1817.
49	"	Isaac Senter,	March 28, 1820.
3	BARKER	James (the fourth of the name in lineal descent), son of James and Mary, Dec. 30, 1700.	
3	"	Phebe of James and Mary,	Feb. 17, 1702-3.
3	"	Mary,	April ——, 1705.
3	"	Mary, 2d,	May 9, 1706.
3	"	Priscilla,	July 26, 1708.
3	"	John,	Dec. 18, 1710.

8	BARKER Robert, of James and Mary,	June 12, 1712.
3	" Sarah,	Dec. 30, 1714.
3	" Peleg,	July 11, 1716.
3	" Phebe, 2d,	Nov. 14, 1717.
3	" Deborah,	Jan. 17, 1720.
177	" Phebe, aged 8 years,	d. Sept. ——, 1710.
177	" Mary, aged 3 months,	d. July ——, 1705.
177	" Sarah, aged 9 months,	d. Sept. ——, 1715.
8	" Sarah, of Jeremiah and Penelope,	April 5, 1725.
8	" Caleb,	Nov. 1, 1726.
8	" Joshua,	Nov, 1, 1726.
8	" Priscilla,	Nov. 24, 1728.
8	" Mary,	Oct. 3, 1730.
8	" Jeremiah,	Feb. 24, 1732.
8	" Edward,	April 13, 1736.
8	" Penelope,	April 22, ——.
8	" Susanna,	June 29, 1744.
8	" James (the fifth of the name by lineal descent), son of James and Mary, Dec. 12, 1725.	
8	" John, of James and Mary,	Aug. 30, 1732.
4	" Edward, of Robert and Phebe,	June 25, 1734.
6, 45	" Hezekiah, of John and Rebecca,	Aug. 24, 1736.
45	" Hezekiah,	d. May 21, 1755.
6, 45	" Mary,	May 19, 1738.
45	" Mary,	d. March 3, 1750-1.
6, 45	" John,	Aug. 8, 1841.
45	" John,	d. Sept. 21, 1745.
6, 45	" Elisha,	June 27, 1744.
45	" John.	Dec. 27, 1746.
15, 45	" David,	Dec. 4, 1751.
15, 45	" Samuel.	April 7, 1754.
15, 45	" Hezekiah,	April 14, 1757.
4	" Robert, of Robert and Sarah,	Jan. 7, 1738-9.
4	" George,	Oct. 7, 1744.
10	" Phebe,	May 14, 1746.
20	" Sarah,	Aug. 4, 1748.
20	" Robert,	Jan. 13, 1750.
8	" Patience, of William, Jr., and Mary,	Aug. 31, 1745.
177	" John, of John and Rebecca, died aged about 4 years, Sept. 27, 1745.	
10	" John, of John and Rebecca,	Dec. 27, 1746.
15	" William, of William and Mary,	Sept. 29, 1746.
15	" Joseph,	Feb. 12, 1748.
176	" Joseph,	d. June 1, 1749.
16	" Ann,	March 21, 1749-50.
15, 31	" James, of James, Jr., and Anne,	Nov. 1, 1749.
24, 31	" Isaac.	May 21, 1752.
31	" Silas	Jan. 6, 1756.
31	" Ezra	Nov. 4, 1759.
31	" Paul,	Aug. 20, 1762.
31	" Henry,	Jan. 31, 1766.
31	" Peckham,	Dec. 28, 1767.
31	" Mary,	Feb. 24, 1770.
176	" Robert, of Robert, and Sarah, d. Nov. 11, 1750.	
176	" Sarah, wife of Robert, died, aged between 34 and 35 years, Jan. 26, 1750.	
176	" Mary, of John and Rebecca, died, aged 12y. 9m. 12d., March 3, 1750-1.	
27	" Sanford, of Robert and Frances,	Dec. 18, 1753.
115	" Peleg, of Peter and Ruth,	Sept. 21, 1753.
115	" Mary (ward of Richard and Elizabeth) his wife, June 13, 1758.	
115	" Catharine, of Peleg and Mary,	May 20, 1785.
115	" Ruth L.,	Sept. 3, 1787.
115	" Abraham.	Jan. 14, 1794.
115	" Peleg L.,	Sept. 11, 1796.

115	BARKER Eliphal, of Peleg and Mary,	Sept. 11, 1798.
115	" Benajah,	Feb. 10, 1801.
115	" Rhoda,	April 9, 1803.
176	" Hezekiah, of John and Rebecca, drowned, aged 18y. 9m., May 21, 1765.	
107	" Matthew, of Peter, Jr., dec., May 21, 1756.	
107	" Eunice, his wife, Dec. 23, 1761.	
107	" Arnold, of Matthew and Eunice,	March 14, 1780.
107	" Giles.	Dec. 20, 1781.
107	" Sarah,	Nov. 11, 1783.
107	" Ruth,	Oct. 1, 1785.
107	" Peter,	June 25, 1787.
107	" Mary,	May 2, 1789.
107	" Joseph Peckham.	Jan. 4, 1790.
176	" Mary, wife of James, died, aged about 79 years, Feb. 24, 1758.	
176	" James, died in 83d year, March 27, 1758.	
99	" Benedict, of Edward and Alice,	Sept. 14, 1767.
53	" Jethro, of Elisha and Phebe,	March 6, 1769.
53	" Jethro,	d. Dec. 6, 1771.
53	" Mary.	Aug. 27, 1772.
53	" Nathan.	Oct. 1, 1774.
53	" Arnold.	April 7, 1777.
58	" John Holmes, of Joshua and Hannah.	April 4, 1769.
58	" Anne,	Feb. 9, 1772.
58	" Isaac.	Aug. 1, 1773.
58	" Joshua,	Sept. 16, 1775.
68	" Cynthia, of James, 3d, and Rhoda.	Nov. 6, 1771.
68	" James (the seventh of the name)	April 9, 1773.
68	" John, of David and Eunice,	Oct. 1, 1773.
68	" John,	d. Sept. 8, 1777.
68	" Rebecca,	Aug. 23, 1774.
68	" Christopher.	May 28, 1776.
68	" John,	Dec. 19, 1777.
68	" George,	March 1, 1779.
68	" Gideon,	Aug. 1, 1780.
68	" Nancy,	Aug. 2, 1782.
68	" David,	May 23, 1784.
68	" Eliphaz,	July 6, 1786.
68	" Rachel,	Feb. 27, 1788.
68	" Sarah,	Jan. 30, 1790.
68	" Simon,	July 9, 1791.
68	" Elijah,	Aug. 31, 1793.
68	" Hezekiah,	Dec. 26, 1796.
68	" Charles,	Jan. 2, 1799.
71	" Anna, of Isaac and Sarah,	Oct. 28, 1776.
71	" Anna,	d. Sept. 26, 1778.
71	" Stephen,	Oct. 26, 1779.
71	" Job,	July 19, 1781.
71	" Dorcas,	Dec. 14, 1782.
71	" James,	Dec. 28, 1784.
71	" James, 2d,	April 29, 1792.
71	" Hiram,	March 7, 1794.
112	" Giles, of Matthew,	Dec. 20, 1783.
112	" Lillis, wife of Giles,	Feb. 26, 1786.
112	" Mary, of Giles and Lillis,	June 16, 1804.
112	" Elizabeth,	Oct. 2, 1805.
112	" Samuel Sanford,	April 4, 1808.
91	" Nathaniel, of Gideon and Elizabeth,	Nov. 14, 1782.
91	" Cynthia,	Feb. 10, 1787.
96	" Elizabeth, of Samuel and Sarah,	July 8, 1783.
96	" Samuel Smith,	Feb. 15, 1793.
96	" William, (b. Newport),	Feb. 4, 1798.
35	" Cyrus, of Isaac and Sarah,	Aug. 20, 1786.
35	" Ira,	Aug. 7, 1788.
175	" James,	d. Jan. 5, 1788.

175	BARKER Eunice, wife of Matthew, died (dau. of James Peckham), Oct. 14, 1792.	
111	" Eliza, of Nathaniel and Mary,	Oct. 28, 1804.
11	" Mary Croad,	Oct. 19, 1806.
111	" John Croad,	Oct. 7, 1808.
111	" Angelina,	Oct. 1, 1810.
139	" Ann, of John and Dorcas,	April 10, 1807.
139	" Albert,	Sept. 12, 1808.
139	" Ruth H.,	Jan. 15, 1811.
139	" Job M.,	May 3, 1812.
139	" Lucinda,	Nov. 17, 1813.
139	" Robinson P.,	Aug. 25, 1816.
139	" Benedict,	Jan. 10, 1818.
140	" Matilda P., of James and Ruth.	Feb. 14, 1815.
140	" Paul,	Nov. 29, 1817.
140	" Joseph O.,	June 27, 1819.
140	" Roxanna,	July 6, 1821.
140	" Dorcas A.,	Feb. 26, 1823.
140	" Hiram,	Sept. 5, 1826.
140	" Ezra J.,	April 18, 1829.
154	" William, of James and Eliphal,	Jan. 14, 1834.
167	" John P., of Albert G. and Mary Ann,	July 13, 1836.
167	" Mary Ann Weaver, of Albert G. and Mary, 2d wife, Oct, 19, 1844.	
167	" Dorcas E.,	Sept. 13, 1847.
167	" Mumford Peckham,	March 29, 1853.
167	" Clarke Taggart,	March 29, 1853.
167	" James T., of Job M. and Julia M.,	Nov. 9, 1838.
167	" Julia M.,	Dec. 4, 1839.
167	" Ann M.,	Aug. 13, 1841.
167	" Jacob J.,	Oct. 12, 1843.
167	" Washington S.,	May 15, 1847.
167	" Josephine L.,	Nov. 1, 1849.
168	" Stephen, of Joseph O., and Hannah M.,	Sept. 30, 1844.
168	" Adoniram J.,	Oct. 31, 1846.
168	" Luther B.,	April 12, 1850.
168	" Edgar,	May 17. 1854.
33	BLISS Elizabeth, of William and Barbara,	June 25, 1750.
33	" Barbara,	Oct. 20, 1751.
33	" Amey.	Jan. 16, 1753.
33	" Arnold,	July 16, 1754.
33	" Mary,	Jan. 15, 1757.
33	" William,	July 22, 1758.
33	" John,	Jan. 7, 1760.
33	" Thomas Ward,	June 2, 1761.
33	" George,	Oct. 19, 1763.
33	" Sarah.	Oct. 15, 1765.
33	" Josiah,	Dec. 30, 1767.
33	" Jeremiah,	March 4, 1770.
22	BROWN Alce, of Nicholas and Mary,	June 20, 1737.
22	" Mary,	April 26, 1739.
22	" Tobias.	Sept. 22, 1741.
22	" Nicholas,	Nov. 1, 1743.
22	" Benjamin,	May 1, 1746.
22	" Ruth.	Nov. 9, 1748.
22	" Ruamy,	Aug. 19, 1751.
27	" William, of William and Judith,	July 1, 1743.
27	" Priscilla,	Aug. 24, 1744.
27	" Gideon,	Sept. 18, 1745.
27	" Elizabeth,	Jan. 25, 1746.
27	" Ruth.	June 6, 1748.
27	" Sarah.	March 26, 1752.
27	" Pardon,	Nov. 18, 1754.
27	" Peleg,	April 28, 1757.
27	" Lydia,	Feb. 23, 1759.
27	" James.	Jan. 5, 1761.
27	" Palmer.	July 9, 1762.

62	BROWN William, of William and Mary	Aug. 16, 1766.
62	"	Abigail,	Nov. 27, 1767.
62	"	Alice,	Sept. 3, 1769.
62	"	John Coggeshall,	Jan. 12, 1771.
62	"	Mary,	March —, 1772.
62	"	Elizabeth,	Feb. 12, 1774.
62	"	Thurston,	Dec. 2, 1777.
62	"	James,	Jan. 21, 1780.
59	"	Mary, of Gideon and Sarah,	June 8, 1768.
59	"	Ruth,	Nov 4, 1769.
59	"	Gideon,	Sept. 15, 1771.
59	"	Elizabeth,	May 15, 1773.
63	"	Mary, of Gideon and Sarah,	June 8, 1769.
63	"	Ruth,	Nov. 4, 1770.
94	"	Thomas, of Peleg and Mary,	Jan. 5, 1779.
94	"	Mercy,	Nov. 5, 1780.
94	"	Joseph,	Sept. 7, 1782.
94	"	Judith,	May 21, 1784.
94	"	Peleg,	March 3, 1786.
94	"	Palmer,	Dec. 8, 1787.
94	"	Anne,	May 3, 1790.
94	"	William Coggeshall,	April 11, 1792.
94	"	James Hale,	July 31, 1794.
94	"	George Coggeshall,	Dec. 2, 1798.
94	"	Pardon,	Dec. 24, 1801.
94	"	Joshua Coggeshall,	Dec. 24, 1801.
94	"	Robert Dennis,	March 22, 1805.
125	"	Emeline, of George and Elizabeth,	Jan. 30, 1809.
125	"	Edwin Gardiner,	Dec. 26, 1810.
125	"	Elizabeth Peckham,	Dec. 19, 1812.
125	"	William,	Feb. 26, 1815.
131	"	George Washington, of Abraham and Lucy,	May 17, 1821.
131	"	Charles Feke,	Feb, 20, 1823.
131	"	Mary Burr,	Nov. 20, 1825.
131	"	Lydia Briggs,	Oct. 14, 1826.
131	"	Abraham Freeman,	Sept. 27, 1828.
131	"	Lucy Electa,	March 24, 1831.
124	"	George Armstrong, of Pardon and Lucy,	Oct. 4, 1822.
124	"	Pardon,	Jan. 5, 1825.
172	"	Abraham, of William, died	July 31, 1830.
173	BUFFUM Elder David, died aged 85 y., 5 m., 8 d.,	5m., 20th, 1729.

C

48	CARD Sarah, of John and Sarah,	May 27, 1765.
51	CHAPMAN Edward, of Edward and Ruth,	Oct. 28, 1766.
52	CHASE Isaac, of James and Lydia,	June 10, 1765.
108	"	Aaron, of Royal and Ruth,	8m 3d.,1793.
108	"	Eliza,	3m. 11d., 1795.
108	"	Peter,	5m. 31d., 1797.
108	"	Perry,	6m. 16d., 1799.
108	"	William,	8m. 22d., 1802.
108	"	Darius,	12m. 4d., 1804.
171	"	Alfred Whitman, of John and Sarah,	April 7, 1835.
171	"	Mary Jane,	March 11, 1837.
171	"	Mary Jane,	d. July 2, 1849.
171	"	Maria Louisa,	Dec. 6, 1838.
171	"	Rebecca Coggeshall,	Aug. 21, 1843.
171	"	Rebecca Coggeshall,	d. April 14, 1847.
171	"	Harriet Amelia,	Aug. 26, 1845.
171	"	Harriet Amelia,	d. April 18, 1847.
171	"	Henry Jackson,	July 29, 1850.
171	"	son, (still born),	Jan 8, 1852.

169	CHASE	Elizabeth Coggeshall, of George G. and Hannah M ,	Feb. 24, 1844.
169	"	Elizabeth Coggeshall,	d. Feb. 11, 1852.
169	"	Mary Allen,	Feb. 24, 1846.
169	"	Joshua Coggeshall,	April 6, 1848.
169	"	Joshua Coggsshall,	d. June 4, 1849.
169	"	Anna Hazard,	Nov. 17, 1853.
169	"	Emma Gould,	July 31, 1858.
143	"	George, of Robert S. and Amarentha,	Sept. 17, 1847.
143	"	William James,	Oct. 20, 1849.
144	"	Peleg Coggeshall, of William B., and Cynthia,	Sept. 20, 1849.
144	"	Anna B.,	July 20, 1852.
39	CHURCH	Sarah, of Constant and Hannah,	Jan 27, 1757.
39	"	Constant,	Feb. 10, 1759.
13	CLARKE	Joseph, of Lawrence,	Sept. 29, 1713.
13	"	Elizabeth, (Spooner), his wife,	Oct. 12, 1721.
13	"	James, of Joseph and Elizabeth,	Jan. 29, 1740.
13	"	Rebecca,	Jan. 18, 1741.
13	"	Mary,	June 30, 1743.
13	"	Joseph,	April 25, 1745.
7	"	George, of John and Priscilla,	Dec. 4, 1729.
7	"	James,	Aug. 24, 1731.
7	"	Frances,	June 4, 1734.
7	"	Phebe,	May 11, 1736.
7	"	Priscilla,	May 7, 1738.
7	"	Jeremiah,	Sept. 14, 1744.
7	"	John,	Nov. 9, 1742.
7	"	Mary,	Oct. 11, 1744.
177	"	George,	d. Oct. 30, 1732.
177	"	Priscilla,	d. June 20, 1738.
177	"	Mary,	d. Oct. 2, 1745.
7	"	Sarah, of Lawrence and Lydia,	July 7, 1734.
7	"	Hannah,	Nov. 20, 1735.
7	"	Jonathan,	Dec. 6, 1737.
7	"	Lydia,	April 20, 1740.
7	"	William,	Nov. 18, 1742.
7	"	Ann,	March 17, 1744-5.
13	"	Elizabeth, of Stephen and Bathsheba,	Nov. 25, 1738.
13	"	Phebe,	Sept. 9, 1741.
13	"	Benjamin,	Feb. 6, 1743.
13	"	Joseph,	Dec. 12, 1747.
9	"	Ann, of Cornelius and Patience,	July 5, 1743.
10	"	Ruth,	Dec. 6, 1744.
176	"	Elizabeth, wife of Joseph, died aged about 25 years,	June 27, 1746.
20	"	Priscilla, of John and Priscilla,	June 16, 1746.
20	"	George,	Oct. 13, 1748.
20	"	Weston,	Nov. 15, 1749.
20	"	Walter,	Sept. 21, 1751.
10	"	Elizabeth, of Lawrence and Lydia,	May 30, 1747.
19	"	Spooner, of Joseph and Phebe,	July 31, 1750.
24	"	Lawrence, of Stephen and Bathsheba,	May 9, 1752.
175	"	Priscilla, wife of John. died aged 55 years,	Feb. 16, 1764.
57	"	Samuel, of Jeremiah and Elizabeth,	Sept. 3, 1770.
57	"	Abigail,	May 25, 1772.
57	"	Latham,	Aug. 31, 1774.
57	"	Sarah Cook,	Jan. 10, 1776.
72	"	Peleg, of Walter and Lydia,	Nov. 20, 1775.
72	"	Weston,	Feb. 24, 1784.
72	"	Francis,	July 8, 1787.
72	"	Prescilla,	March 3, 1789.
72	"	Mehitable,	April 21, 1791.
72	"	Walter,	July 28, 1793.
174	"	2d. dau. of Samuel and Ruth,	d. March —, 1783.
174	"	Ruth, wife of Samuel,	d. July 6, 1801.
174	"	Virtue, wife of Samuel,	d. May 22, 1801.
174	"	Ruth, wife of Samuel,	d. Dec. 1, 1808.

108	CLARKE	John, of Weston and Phebe,	Aug. 14, 1802.
108	"	Hannah Howard.	Sept. 20, 1804.
108	"	Benjamin Howard,	June 2, 1807.
108	"	William Shandley,	March 24, 1810.
92	"	Mary Ann, of Jedde and Mary,	April 29, 1808.
21	COGGESHALL	Elizabeth, of Thomas and Mercy,	Aug. 20, 1710.
21	"	Comfort.	Sept. 17, 1712.
21	"	Mercy,	June 30, 1714.
21	"	Sarah,	Aug. 20, 1715.
21	"	Wait.	Jan. 4, 1717.
21	"	Mary.	March 27, 1720.
21	"	Joshua, 2d,	May 11, 1722.
21	"	Mercy, 2d,	Feb. 3, 1723-4.
22	"	Gideon.	April 30, 1726.
22	"	Thomas,	Aug. 26, 1728.
22	"	Hannah.	May 20, 1731.
4, 46	"	Thomas, of Joshua and Sarah,	Aug. 30, 1744.
4, 46	"	Ruth,	June 26, 1747.
30, 46	"	Sarah, of Joshua and Anne, 2d wife,	Sept. 25. 1752.
30, 46	"	Joseph.	Aug. 16, 1754.
30, 46	"	Elizabeth.	Oct. 14, 1756.
30, 46	"	George.	March 17, 1759.
30, 46	"	Mary,	July 14, 1761.
30, 46	"	Mercy,	Sept. 14, 1762.
46	"	Anne.	June 1, 1764.
33	"	James, of James and Phebe,	May 25, 1746.
22	"	Gideon, of Gideon and Hannah,	April 16, 1751.
28	"	John, of Thomas and Hannah,	May 7, 1751.
28	"	Josiah.	Aug. 13, 1752.
28	"	William,	Jan. 7, 1757.
28	"	Barbara, of Nicholas and Sarah,	Sept. 19, 175--.
28	"	Alice.	April 16, 1754.
22	"	Timothy, of Gideon, and Hannah,	Aug. 16, 1753.
22	"	Mercy,	Sept. 18, 1755.
22, 40	"	Thomas,	Jan. 8, 1759.
175	"	George, of Joshua, and Ann,	d. Nov. 16, 1762.
62	"	Jonathan, of Jonathan, and Sarah,	April 19, 1767.
62	"	Catherine,	April 23, 1768.
62	"	Wealthian,	April 15, 1770.
62	"	Mehitable,	Aug. 25, 1772.
44	"	John Bailey, of Thomas, and Hester,	June 29, 1774.
70	"	Samuel, of John and Sarah,	Aug. 16, 1774.
70	"	Thurston,	Feb. 21, 1780.
87	"	Noel, of Joseph and Elizabeth,	Mar. 31. 1777.
87	"	Ruth.	Aug. 27, 1780.
87	"	Joseph,	June 5, 1783.
87	"	Anne,	Jan. 28, 1786.
87	"	Joshua,	Dec. 26, 1788.
87	"	Sarah,	Sept. 18, 1791.
87	"	John P.,	April 13, 1794.
87	"	Abraham,	Mar. 15, 1797.
23	"	Jonathan, of James, and Phebe,	Dec. 4, 1748.
114	"	Asa, of Thomas and Hester,	Nov. 4, 1783.
114	"	Sarah, (Barker, of Matthew and Eunice), his wife,	Nov. 11, 1783.
114	"	Eunice, of Asa and Sarah,	Mar. 31, 1802.
114	"	Arnold,	Jan. 25, 1804.
114	"	Peter,	June 19, 1806.
114	"	Asa,	Oct. 9, 1808.
93	"	Charles Sherman, of Jonathan, Jr., and Bathsheba,	Sept. 22, 1792.
45	"	Peleg, of John Bailey, and Mary,	Aug. 31, 1795.
45	"	Thomas,	Jan. 22, 1798.
170	"	Caroline C., of Jonathan and Bathsheba, b. Portsmouth, July 14, 1808.	
162	"	George C., of Joshua, Jr., and Deborah,	Oct. 7, 1816.
165	"	David,	Oct. 28, 1818.

162	COGGESHALL Hannah Mary, of Joshua, Jr., and Deborah,	Jan. 6, 1820.
162	" Anne Elizabeth,	Nov. 2, 1822.
162	" Sarah Dennis,	Sept. 21, 1924.
174	" Thomas, died in his 86th year,	Oct. 9, 1829.
172	" Joseph, of Joshua, died, aged 76y., 1m., 20d.,	Oct. 7, 1830.
172	" Ruth, of Joseph and Elizabeth, died, aged 87 years 20 days, Sept. 15, 1867.	
10	CORNELL Ebenezer, of George, Jr., and Mary,	July 18, 1738.
10	" Mehitable,	Dec. 27, 1740.
10	" William,	Jan. 16, 1743-4.
47	" Hannah, of George and Rebecca,	Dec. 29, 1739.
47	" Deliverance,	July 3, 1742.
47	" Robert,	April 5, 1745.
47	" Ruth,	June 20, 1747.
47	" Benjamin,	Sept. 5, 1751.
47	" Patience,	March 26, 1750.
47	" Samuel,	Feb. 24, 1754.
47	" Patience, 2d,	Nov. 12, 1756.
47	" Oliver,	March 29, 1760.
22	" Seth, of George, Jr., and Mary,	July 19, 1751.
28	" Ruth,	Jan. 10, 1754.
33	" Elizabeth,	Dec. 29, 1756.
64	" Anne, of Robert and Hannah,	March 5, 1771.
64	" Hannah,	Aug. 1, 1773.
64	" Rebecca,	Jan. 23, 1775.
64	" Sarah, of Robert and Ruth,	Sept. 28, 1780.
64	" George,	July 9, 1782.
64	" Elizabeth,	Nov. 23, 1784.
103	" Oliver, of Oliver and Hannah,	Oct. 11, 1794.
64	" Robert B., of Gideon and Anne,	Nov. 18, 1801.
64	" Clarke,	Dec. 5, 1803.
129	" George, of Hicks and Elizabeth,	Nov. 11, 1819.

D

110	DAWLEY William W., of Sprague and Lucy,	Dec. 8, 1801.
110	" Paul W.,	March 13, 1802.
110	" Benjamin R.,	Sept. 17, 1803.
110	" Tanary,	June 17, 1805.
110	" George Sprague,	Jan. 10, 1808.
110	" Lucian,	May 18, 1809.
110	" Lydia,	Sept. 10, 1810.
110	" Nicholas Taylor,	June 27, 1811.
110	" Hannah,	Feb. 11, 1814.
110	" Horatius Nelison,	March 9, 1815.
110	" Oliver H. P.,	Feb. 4, 1816.
110	" Wightman,	Oct. 25, 1818.
13	DILLINGHAM Hannah, of Cornelius and Sarah,	Sept. 2, 1748.
14	DRING Caroline, of Freelove,	Sept. 14, 1745.
28	DURFEE Oliver, of Thomas and Mary,	Feb. 27, 1754.
55	" Mary, of James and Ruth,	Sept. 21, 1763.
55	" Rebecca,	Feb. 16, 1765.
55	" Benjamin,	May 18, 1767.
55	" Elizabeth,	April 21, 1769.
55	" James,	Aug. 11, 1777.
107	" Ruth, of Benjamin, Jr., and Elizabeth,	Dec. 3, 1790.
107	" Rebecca,	Sept. 19, 1792.
107	" Lydia Stanton,	Sept. 19, 1794.
107	" Mary,	Sept. 21, 1796.
107	" Hannah Beebe,	Sept. 3, 1798.
107	" Raymond,	Dec. 8, 1801.
107	" Katharine Stanton,	Sept. 30, 1803.
55	" Jesse Tripp, of James, Jr., and Mary,	Aug. 18, 1800.
55	" Eliza Seabury,	May 11, 1802.

56	DURFEE Timothy Pearce, of James, Jr., and Mary,	Jan. 5, 1804.
81	" Isaac P.,	Dec. 9, 1805.
81	" Mary Ann,	Oct. 4, 1807.
81	" Mary Ann,	d. Feb. 12, 1810.
81	" Ruth 8.,	May 28, 1809.
81	" Mary,	Dec. 23, 1811.
81	" Josephine,	March 18, 1819.
100	DYER Charles, of James, (b. Little Compton),	March 22, 1697.
100	" James, of Charles and Elizabeth (b. Little Compton), Jan. 10, 1727.	
40	" Deborah, of James and Elizabeth	Jan. 27, 1759.
40	" Elizabeth,	May 29, 1763.
40	" Edward (b. Philadelphia, Pa.),	Aug. 27, 1767.
40	" Aaron, of Edward and Abigail (b. Portsmouth),	Jan. 19, 1800.

E

69	EASTON Nicholas, of Jonathan and Patience,	Sept. 16, 1733.
3	" Edward, of Edward and Ruth,	Jan. 28, 1737-8.
9	" Ann, of Peleg and Ann,	Oct. 18, 1743.
9	" Ann, 2d,	Nov. 24, 1745.
177	" Ann, of Edward and Ruth, aged, 3w. 1d.,	d. Dec. 15, 1745.
13	" Joshua, of Peter and Ann,	Feb. 24, 1746-7.
40	" Edward, of Edward and Elizabeth,	Aug. 24, 1761.
40	" Ruth,	Feb. 21, 1763.
69	" Patience, of Nicholas and Hannah (b. Portsmouth),	April 2, 1771.
69	" Hannah,	Feb. 12, 1773.
69	" Jonathan,	July 6, 1774.
69	" Jonathan,	d. Jan. 1, 1775.
69	" Mary,	Dec. 2, 1775.
69	" Sarah,	June 27, 1778.
69	" Nancy,	Aug. 16, 1780.
69	" Elizabeth,	Oct. 27, 1782.
69	" Harriet,	April 18, 1786.
60	" Maria, of William and Sarah (now Sarah Hull),	May 7, 1788.
26	EDDY Anne, of Job and Patience,	Oct. 18, 1748.
32	" Ezekiel, of Primus and Sarah (free negro),	Nov. 10, 1756.

F

34	FREEBORN Gideon, of Noel and Philis,	Feb. 20, 1757.

G

127	GARDINER Benjamin, of John, of South Kingstown, Jan. 4, 1750.	
127	" Elizabeth (Weekes, of Thomas, of Norwich), ———.	
127	" Thomas, of Benjamin and Elizabeth (b. Boston Neck, North Kingstown),	June 20, 1775; d. Aug. 11, 1775.
127	" Weekes, of Benjamin and Elizabeth (b. Tower Hill, South Kingstown),	Sept. 12, 1777.
127	" Benjamin, of Benjamin and Elizabeth (b. Boston Neck, North Kingstown),	Aug. 3, 1779, d. Aug. 3, 1780.
127	" Elizabeth, of Benjamin and Elizabeth,(b. North Kingstown), Aug. 3, 1781; d. at Middletown, May 29, 1786.	
127	" Ruth, of Benjamin and Elizabeth,	Aug. 2, 1784.
127	" Albert,	April 25, 1786.
127	" Edwin,	Dec. 9, 1787.
127	" James Sayer,	March 18, 1789.
127	" Benjamin,	Dec. 31, 1790.
127	" still-born dau.,	Oct. 28, 1794.
127	" Elizabeth, wife of Benjamin, d. in her 42 year, May 8, 1796.	
127	" Amey Ann, 2d wife of Benjamin, d. Jan. 5, 1800.	
127	" still-born dau., of Benjamin and Mary.	Sept.—, 1802.
127	" John Howland,	Jan. 23, 1805.

127	GARDINER Edwin, drowned at sea on passage from Lisbon to Liverpool, Jan. 23, 1805.		
2	GOULD Abigail, of Daniel and Mary,		Nov. 19, 1720.
2	" Priscilla,		Aug. 15, 1722.
2	" Daniel,		Jan. 20, 1723-4.
2	" Mary,		Jan. 1, 1726-7.
2	" Jeremiah,		Nov. 1, 1728.
2	" Thomas,		Feb. 25, 1730-1.
2	" Anne,		May 29, 1733.
2	" Wait,		Jan. 3, 1735-6.
2	" Bathsheba,		July 28, 1738.
177	" Jeremiah, aged 14 years,		d. March 24, 1742-3.
116	" Henrietta, of Thomas and Anna,		Oct. 20, 1791.
116	" Charles,		April 20, 1794.
116	" Son,		Dec. 22, 1796.
116	" Son,		d. Dec. 24, 1796.
116	" Samuel,		Nov. 17, 1799.
116	" Catherine,		June 15, 1801.
116	" Sarah,		Sept. 6, 1804.
116	" Susannah,		Oct. 25, 1807.
116	" John,		Nov. 19, 1810.
116	" James Coggeshall,		June 18, 1814.
116	" Robert,		May 16, 1818.
144	" Mary, of John and Mary,		Feb. 5, 1814.
118	" Emeline, of James and Sarah.		Oct. 3, 1816.
118	" Albert,		June 6, 1818.
118	" Jane,		May 3, 1820.
146	" Jesse, of John and Mary,		June 1, 1822.
146	" Jesse, of John and Mary,		d. Sept. 21, 1833.
8	GREENE Mary, of William and Mary,		April 13, 1730.
8	" William,		June 17, 1732.
47	" William, of William and Sarah,		Dec. 1, 1763.

H

74	HALL Sarah, of Parker and Ruth,		March 21, 1782.
74	" John Bailey,		Jan. 20, 1784.
126	" William P., of Bailey and Sarah,		Jan. 17, 1813.
126	" Juliann,		July 3, 1814.
126	" John B.,		July 11, 1816.
126	" Lucinda,		March 20, 1818.
126	" Harriet Barker,		Sept. 21, 1823.
20	HOAR Sarah, of Hezekiah and Deborah,		Aug. 18, 1739.
20	" Hezekiah,		May 13, 1741.
49	HOLMES John, July 14, 1737,		
49	" Mary, his wife, June 11, 1738.		
49	" Sarah, of John and Mary,		Nov. 19, 1756.
78	HOPKINS Elizabeth, of Thomas and Phebe,		Sept. 23, 1771.
78	" William,		Feb. 25, 1774.
78	" Arnold,		July 27, 1778.
78	" Isaac,		Feb. 26, 1781.
78	" Thomas,		Dec. 25, 1785.
87	" Mary Ann, of John and Sarah,		Aug. 27, 1799.

I

34	IRISH Hannah, of Benjamin and Martha,		Sept. 28, 1780.

J K

39	KIRBY Perry, of John and Ruth,		June 22, 1759.
39	" Ruth,		July 18, 1760.

L

109	LAKE	William, of Benjamin and Elizabeth,	Aug. 24, 1789.
109	"	Benjamin,	Aug. 19, 1791.
110	"	Holder,	Oct. 9, 1793.
110	"	Phebe,	March 21, 1796.
110	"	Mary,	March 15, 1798.
110	"	Jonathan,	April 8, 1800.
110	"	Eliza,	March 20, 1802.
110	"	Arnold,	June 11, 1804.
110	"	Charlotta,	April 23, 1806.
110	"	Abraham,	March 16, 1808.
110	"	Isaac,	April 24, 1810.
110	"	Jacob,	Oct. 31, 1812.
110	"	Thurston,	June 7, 1816.
12	LITTLE	Edward, of Nicholas and Mary,	Nov. 22, 1724.
12	"	Job,	Aug. 22, 1726.
12	"	John,	Jan. 6, 1728.
12	"	William,	Feb. 13, 1730.
12	"	James,	March 5, 1732.
12	"	Nichols,	July 11, 1734.
12	"	Mary,	July 18, 1736.
12	"	Ann,	Sept. 7, 1738.
12	"	Hannah,	June 11, 1741.

M

21	MANCHESTER	Lydia, of Isaac and Hannah,	Sept. 8, 1746.
21	"	John,	Dey. 2, 1748.
21	"	Elizabeth,	Jan. 18, 1751.
21	"	Thomas,	April 27, 1753.
21	"	William,	Aug. 10, 1755.
36, 44	"	Joseph,	Sept. 27, 1757.
44	"	Samuel,	Feb. 6, 1760.
44	"	Isaac,	Aug. 19, 1762.
44	"	Hannah,	March 24, 1764.
44	"	Giles,	Nov. 10, 1766.
75	"	Benjamin, of Isaac, Jr., and Phebe,	Aug. 29, 1786.
75	"	Peter,	Nov. 19, 1788.
83	"	Lydia, of Thomas and Mercy,	March 31, 1787.
83	"	Sarah,	May 12, 1789.
83	"	Isaac,	Feb. 9, 1792.
83	"	Freeborn,	Nov. 14, 1793.
83	"	Anne,	Dec. 12, 1795.
83	"	Hannah,	Nov. 8, 1797.
83	"	Mercy,	March 19, 1800.
83	"	George,	April 22, 1804.
89	"	Mary, of John and Sarah,	March 19, 1788.
89	"	Hannah,	April 2, 1790.
85	"	Katherine Hunter, of William and Ennice,	May 2, 1788.
85	"	Charles,	Sept. 19, 1789.
85	"	Elizabeth,	Nov. 12, 1792.
84	"	Alfred, of Joseph and Hannah,	Oct. 24, 1788.
96	"	Sarah,	July 25, 1792.
96	"	John,	Sept. 9, 1790.
96	"	David Greene,	April 10, 1794.
102	"	Eliza, of Samuel and Mehitable,	Oct. 17, 1800.
102	"	Samuel,	April 26, 1802.
102	"	Mary Ann,	April 25, 1805.
113	"	Sarah Ann, of Freeborn and Ann,	Nov. 12, 1818.
113	"	Stephen,	March 16, 1820.
113	"	George Tew,	May 23, 1823.
113	"	Truman,	Nov. 13, 1825.
113	"	Peter A.,	May 19, 1835.

134	MANCHESTER Cook, of Isaac and Sally,	Aug. 2, 1823.
134	" Freeborn,	July 5, 1825.
38	MARTIN James, of George and Barbara,	Dec. 25, 1739.
38	" Thomas,	Sept. 10, 1741.
38	" Joseph,	May 17, 1743.
38	" George,	July 27, 1744.
38	" Mary,	April 27, 1746.
38	" Samuel,	Feb. 2, 1748.
38	" Elizabeth,	March 3, 1749.
38	" Albro,	April 17, 1750.
88	" Abigail,	May 17, 1755.
38	" Gideon,	Dec. 26, 1756.

Note.—First, sixth and last two in Middletown; the others Portsmouth.

4	MITCHELL Mary, of James and Anne,	Nov. 16, 1739.
4	" James,	Aug. 31, 1743.
26	" Elizabeth,	July 9, 1746.
26	" Hephsabeth,	March 4, 1750.
31	" Richard,	July 25, 1754.
55	" Mary, of James, Jr., and Rhoda,	Aug. 12, 1767.
57	" Jethro, of Richard and Joanna.	3m., 14th, 1778.
57	" Isaac,	8m., 21st, 1779.
57	" John,	1m., 15th, 1781.
57	" Elizabeth,	Oct. 17, 1782.
57	" Peter,	July 3, 1784.
57	" Sarah,	May 19, 1787.
57	" Joanna,	Dec. 3, 1788.
57	" Anna,	8m., 6th, 1791.
57	" Richard,	2m., 20th, 1793.
92	" Joseph, of Jethro Folgeer and Anne,	4m., 21st, 1802.
92	" James,	3m., 26th, 1804.
175	" James,	d. 4m., 7th, 1805.
53	" Joanna, of John and Katharine,	2m., 12th, 1807.
53	" Sarah,	9m., 12th, 1808.
53	" Lydia,	9m., 1st, 1810.
53	" John,	7m., 25th, 1812.
53	" Catherine,	10m., 22nd, 1814.
53	" Lucy,	10m., 2d, 1817.
53	" Julia Ann,	1m. 29d. 1820.
92	" Rebecca Gould, of Isaac and Sarah,	4m., 8d. 1808.

N O

16	NICHOLS Jonathan, of Robert and Alice,	Dec. 20, 1738.
16	" Ruth,	April 1, 1741.
16	" Sarah,	Aug. 28, 1743.
16	" Elizabeth,	Oct. 5, 1746.
16	" Susannah,	Jan. 23, 1748.
26	" Benjamin,	July 18, 1753.
16	" Hannah,	Aug. 12, 1754.
1	" Elizabeth, of Joseph and Mary,	March 16, 1743-4.
17	" Ann,	June 26, 1746.
17	" Ruth,	May 15, 1748.
19	" John,	Feb. 6, 1750.
26	" Mary,	April 15, 1753.

P

16	PEABODY Joseph, of John and Dorcas,	Nov. 9, 1735.
33	" Caleb, of Joseph and Barbara,	Oct. 25, 1756.
33	" John,	May 19, 1758.
33	" Benjamin,	Nov. 27, 1760.
33	" Mary,	Sept. 26, 1762.
175	" Benjamin, died, aged 2m. 21d,	Feb. 17, 1761.

41	PEABODY Benjamin, 2d, of Joseph and Barbara,	Sept. 26, 1765.
56	" Dorcas,	May 1, 1769.
122	" William Bailey, of William and Sally,	Nov. 6. 1804.
122	" Lionel Henry,	Aug. 1, 1806.
122	" Phebe Ann,	Feb. 10, 1809.
122	" George Alvin,	Aug. 2, 1811.
143	" Ruth, of Easton and Mary,	July 9, 1817.
143	" Hannah,	June 7, 1819.
143	" Silas,	Dec. 4, 1820.
143	" Caroline.	Feb. 1, 1823.
143	" Sarah,	Feb. 1, 1825.
143	" Elizabeth V.,	Oct. 14. 1826.
143	" Joseph Cyrus,	April 6, 1829.
173	" Cobb, died in 73d year, July 29, 1829.	
173	" Anna, wife of Cobb, died in 72d year, July 29, 1823.	
25	PECKHAM Joseph, of Daniel and Comfort,	Dec. 10, 1734.
25	" Elizabeth,	Sept. 3, 1736.
25	" Sarah,	Sept. 29, 1738.
25	" Sarah,	d. April 20, 1741.
25	" Mary,	Sept. 26, 1740.
25	" Sarah, 2d,	March 2, 1743.
25	" Sarah, 2d,	d. Jan. 6, 1751.
25	" Mercy,	June 29, 1746.
25	" Mercy,	d. Jan. 8, 1751.
25	" John,	Sept. 20, 1748.
25	" Patience,	June 26, 1754.
20	" Sarah, of Joshua and Ruth,	Oct. 24, 1741.
176	" Joshua,	d. Oct. 31, 1741.
24	" Martha, of Benjamin and virtue,	June 19, 1746.
24	" Richard,	Aug. 22, 1747.
24	" Ruth,	Oct. 14, 1749.
24	" Mary,	June 10, 1751.
120	" Samuel, April 20, 1751.	
120	" Ruth (Peckham), his wife, Oct. 14, 1749.	
120	" Elizabeth, of Samuel, and Ruth.	Sept. 10, 1774.
120	" Martha,	Nov. 18, 1776.
120	" Virtue,	Aug. 30, 1778.
120	" twins, still-born,	Mar. —, 1783.
120	" Benjamin,	May 23, 1784.
120	" Frances,	Feb. 4, 1787.
120	" Christiana,	Sept. 28, 1789.
120	" Ruth, of Samuel and Virtue, 2d wife,	May 22, 1805.
120	" Virtue, 2d wife of Samuel, born, Feb. 7, 1761.	
26	" Elizabeth, of Samuel and Mary,	Sept. 16, 1752.
26	" Anne,	May 10, 1754.
32	" Samuel,	Oct. 29, 1756.
37	" Levi,	April 17, 1758.
32	" Wealthian,	April 3, 1762.
32	" Isaac,	July 9, 1766.
29	" Benjamin, of Benjamin and Virtue,	Feb. 12, 1753.
29	" Isaac,	March 29, 1755.
29	" Daniel,	Feb. 20, 1758.
35	" Sarah, of Stephen and Naoma,	Aug. 9, 1756.
43	" Joshua, of William and Sarah,	June 18, 1759.
43	" Augustus,	Jan. 6, 1761.
48	" Daniel, of Joseph (of Daniel) and Susanna,	April 8, 1760.
48	" Wait,	Feb. 24, 1762.
48	" Hannah Mumford,	March 30, 1764.
48	" John,	Oct. 20, 1766.
48	" Comfort,	Jan. 30, 1769.
48	" Peleg,	Feb. 7, 1771.
48	" Richard Mumford,	July 31, 1773.
48	" Daniel, 2d,	April 29, 1776.
48	" Joseph,	Sept. 27, 1778.
48	" Caleb Earl,	Oct. 7, 1782.
44	" Virtue, of Benjamin and Virtue,	Feb. 7, 1761.

44	PECKHAM Barbara, of Benjamin and Virtue,	Feb. 7, 1761.
44	" Rhoda,	Feb. 7, 1761.
44	" Rhoda, died same day,	
44	" Nye, of Philip and Jane,	June 11, 1761.
105	" Isaac, of Joseph and Sarah, —— 12, 1763.	
105	" Ruth, his wife (b. East Greenwich), April 16, 1764.	
105	" Catharine, of Isaac and Ruth,	Aug. 28, 1786.
105	" Joseph,	July 28, 1787.
105	" Erasmus Kelley,	Oct. 29, 1788.
105	" Esther,	June 9, 1790.
105	" Auchley,	Feb. 17, 1792.
105	" John,	Feb. 22, 1794.
105	" Ruth,	Nov. 7, 1799.
105	" Isaac,	Dec. 6, 1802.
97	" Alanson, of Joseph, Sept. 20, 1765.	
97	" Catherine, his wife, Aug. 23, 1768.	
97	" Jethro, of Alanson and Catherine,	Nov. 13, 1788.
97	" Jane,	Dec. 13, 1789.
97	" Asa,	Nov. 20, 1791.
97	" Josias,	Nov. 25, 1793.
97	" Eunice,	Dec. 31, 1795.
97	" Catharine,	Oct. 20, 1797.
97	" Jonathan Coggeshall,	July 3, 1799.
97	" Catherine.	April 29, 1802.
97	" Sarah Ann,	Aug. 5, 1804.
97	" Alanson,	May 18, 1806.
97	" Adaline,	May 22, 1808.
97	" Joseph,	April 4, 1810.
97	" Jesse,	April 10, 1812.
61	" William Smith, of Elisha and Mary,	Feb. 26, 1771.
61	" Hannah,	Sept. 11, 1772.
61	" Phebe,	May 12, 1776.
67	" Isaac, of Richard and Elizabeth (Clarke),	March 30, 1773.
67	" Barbara,	Oct. 29, 1774.
67	" Arnold,	April 27, 1776.
67	" Daniel,	Aug. 20, 1778.
67	" Benjamin,	April 18, 1780.
67	" Martha,	May 5, 1782.
67	" Mary Torsey,	Dec. 3, 1784.
67	" Clement,	April 28, 1786.
67	" Henry,	Aug. 27, 1788.
67	" Richard.	July 3, 1791.
67	" Elizabeth. wife of Richard, born May 31, 1747.	
66	" Edward Smith, of Peleg and Elizabeth,	Aug. 1, 1773.
66	" Henry,	Dec. 27, 1780.
66	" Mary,	April 4, 1783.
66	" Peleg,	Oct. 13, 1785.
66	" Elizabeth,	Sept. 10, 1788.
66	" Elisha,	May 5, 1790.
66	" Phebe,	June 21, 1792.
175	" Daniel, eldest son of Daniel and Susanna, died	May 24, 1776.
73	" Peleg Frank, of Thomas and Hannah (b. East Greenwich), Oct. 6, 1779.	
73	"	Sept. 13, 1781.
73	"	Sept. 7, 1783.
66	" Samuel, of Levi and Sarah,	Nov. 12, 1780.
66	" Russell Greene,	May 26, 1783.
66	" Weltha,	March 14, 1785.
66	" Mary,	April 22, 1787.
66	" Perry Mumford,	Aug. 14, 1789
66	" Stephen,	Nov. 21, 1791.
66	" Katharine,	Nov. 19, 1795.
66	" Susannah,	Oct. 16, 1800.
59	" William, of Samuel and Elizabeth,	Aug. 16, 1783.
59	" James,	Dec. 27, 1785.

59	PECKHAM Nancy, of Samuel and Elizabeth,		March 3, 1790.
144	"	William, of John,	Jan. 31, 1796.
144	"	William Francis, of John and Anne,	Dec. 24, 1818.
144	"	Elizabeth Amanda,	March 19, 1823.
124	"	James, of Benjamin and Sarah,	Sept. 20, 1801.
124	"	Joshua,	June 11, 1803.
124	"	Absalom,	March 4, 1805.
124	"	Nathaniel,	Dec. 11, 1806.
124	"	Sarah,	April 27, 1809.
124	"	Benjamin,	May 2, 1811.
124	"	Ephraim Seagar,	July 27, 1813.
124	"	Ann Matilda,	July 13, 1815.
124	"	Reuben,	Oct. 12, 1817.
124	"	George Washington,	Sept. 12, 1819.
137	"	William Smith, Jr.,	Jan. 28, 1802.
137	"	Ruth B., of William Smith, Jr.,	Oct. 9, 1828.
137	"	William Wyatt,	Nov. 30, 1831.
74	"	Joseph Phillips, of Samuel and Sarah,	April 22, 1802.
74	"	Sarah Ann,	July 6, 1803.
74	"	Levi,	April 2, 1805.
74	"	Harriet Gardiner,	Feb. 6, 1807.
74	"	Perry Mumford,	Jan. 4, 1809.
74	"	Benjamin Taylor,	Jan. 6, 1611.
74	"	Mary Ann Durfee,	March 6, 1813.
175	"	Catherine, of Alanson,	d. May 28, 1802.
153	"	Lydia B., of Henry and Esther,	Dec. 1, 1803.
153	"	Henry,	June 17, 1805.
153	"	Edward S.,	June 11, 1807.
153	"	Nicholas Alfred,	June 20, 1809.
153	"	Abby Amelia,	Aug. 14, 1811.
153	"	Esther Gould,	July 21, 1813.
153	"	Elizabeth Gardiner,	June 6, 1815.
153	"	James Monroe,	May 14, 1817.
153	"	Sophia L. R.,	April —, 1819.
153	"	Esther Robbins,	May 11, 1821.
154	"	Reuben Morton,	Sept. 17, 1823.
154	"	Mary Ann Sophia,	Sept. 30, 1825.
154	"	Sarah,	May 6, 1829.
119	"	Eliza Ann, of William W. and Cynthia,	Sept. 5, 1806.
119	"	Tillinghast Bailey,	June 15, 1808.
119	"	Frederick Plumer,	Sept. 14, 1811.
119	"	Easton Cook,	Dec. 10, 1813.
119	"	Cynthia Ann,	Feb. 3, 1816.
121	"	Benedict, of Gideon and Cynthia,	Oct. 19, 1806.
121	"	John Croade,	Feb. 16, 1808.
121	"	Elizabeth,	April 23, 1811.
121	"	Cynthia Ann,	Jan. 16, 1813.
93	"	George Hazard, of George and Elizabeth,	Nov. 13, 1806.
85	"	Harriet, of Daniel and Catherine,	Oct. 1, 1807.
85	"	Julia,	Oct. 16, 1809.
130	"	George Hazard, of Peleg, Jr., and Sophia,	June 22, 1613.
130	"	Peleg, 3d,	Feb. 19, 1815.
130	"	Jane Elizabeth,	Sept. 3, 1824.
142	"	Melinda, of Gideon and Cynthia,	May 24, 1815.
142	"	Gideon Barker,	May 16, 1817.
142	"	Hosea,	Oct. 14, 1819.
142	"	Hosea,	d. Sept. 28, 1824.
142	"	Hosea, 2d,	Dec. 14, 1821.
142	"	Nathaniel,	Aug. 27, 1823.
142	"	Sarah,	June 13, 1827.
142	"	Amelia,	May 8, 1830.
142	"	Philip Mason,	Jan. 1, 1833.
135	"	Gideon Brownell, of Henry, Jr.,	Oct. 24, 1815.
135	"	Elizabeth Dwelly,	Feb. 27, 1816.
135	"	Richard Henry,	March 26, 1820.

135	PECKHAM James Warren, of Gideon and Cynthia,	Aug. 10, 1823.
114	" Phebe Catherine, of Elisha and Eliza D.,	April 16, 1817.
114	" Eliza Almy,	Jan. 3, 1819.
114	" Eliza Almy,	d. March 28, 1822.
114	" Eliza Almy, 2d,	May 20, 1822.
114	" Elisha Clarke.	Nov. 23, 1823.
103	" Josias, of Jonathan C. and Harriet,	March 15, 1823.
138	" Joseph Andrew,	Aug. 27, 1825.
138	" Julia Maria.	Sept. 12, 1827.
152	" Mary Elizabeth, of Restcome and Ruth,	Sept. 19, 1828.
152	" John R..	July 31, 1831.
152	" Christopher Sweet,	April 27, 1834.
162	" William Clarke, of Benedict and Hannah H.,	June 30, 1831.
162	" Cyrus Benedict,	March 20, 1833.
162	" Lydia Clarke,	Oct. 5, 1834.
162	" Phebe Ann.	Dec. 26, 1837.
162	" Gideon Thomas,	July 19, 1840.
170	" Peleg, aged 85 years,	d. April 12, 1833.
166	" Helen Estelle, of John and Hannah,	May 24, 1850.
50	PENDLETON William, of William and Martha,	Dec. 26, 1784.
50	" Nancy,	April 26, 1787.
50	" Elisha.	Feb. 6, 1790.
146	PERRY Mary Dorcas, of Joshua and Sarah P.,	Sept. 28, 1816.
26	PHILLIPS Barbara, of James and Hope,	Sept. 17, 1718.
26	" Patience,	April 6, 1723.
26	" James,	Nov. 14, 1727.
26	" Anne,	Feb. 2, 1729.
39	" James, of James and Alice,	Aug. 14, 1753.
39	" Mercy,	July 29, 1755.
39	" Patience,	March 25, 1758.
102	PITMAN William Weeden, of Isaac and Lydia,	July 16, 1798.
102	" Henry Tew,	Oct. 4, 1803.
102	" Mary Ann,	Feb. 25, 1806.
102	" Phebe Vickery,	March 4, 1810.
102	" Isaac Admiral Charles Eldred,	March 14, 1815.

Q R

13	REED Isaac, of Eleazer and Hannah,	March 23, 1746.
13	" Elizabeth,	Nov. 13, 1748.
55	RICE Freelove, of James and Isabel,	April 23, 1767.
55	" Freelove,	d. June —, 1770.
55	" Freelove, 2d,	Oct. 6, 1770.
11	ROGERS Thomas, of Jeremiah and Patience,	May 9, 1739.
11	" Mary,	March 15, 1740.
11	" Elizabeth,	Aug. 7, 1743.
11	" Sarah,	Nov. 23, 1745.
11	" Ruth,	July 22, 1747.
11	" James,	Nov. 9, 1749.
29	" Daniel, of Phebe,	Nov. 10, 1754.
2	RYDER Gideon, of Joseph and Barbara,	Aug. 8, 1742.
2	" Mary,	Feb. 25, 1743.
46	" Joseph,	Jan. 24, 1745-6.
46	" Gideon,	March 3, 1747-8.
46	" Mary,	Jan. 16, 1749-50.
46	" Rowland,	Feb. 8, 1756.
46	" Barbara,	April 27, 1758.
46	" William,	Sept. 2, 1759.
46	" Elizabeth,	Jan. 26, 1762.
46	" Elizabeth, 2d,	Jan. 12, 1764.
46	" Gideon,	Oct. 16, 1769.
76	" Jonathan, of Joseph and Bathsheba,	Oct. 3, 1778.
76	" Lewis,	April 2, 1780.
76	" Joshua,	May 6, 1785.

76	RYDER Ruth, of Joseph and Bathsheba,	March 4, 1791.
76	" Joseph, of William and Abigail,	Oct. 8, 1784.
76	" Gideon,	Oct. 13, 1786.
76	" Hannah,	Aug. 2, 1788.
76	" William,	Aug. 22, 1790.
76	" Sarah,	Sept. 13, 1792.
79	" Silas,	June 12, 1794.
79	" Abigail,	March 22, 1797.
79	" Caleb,	July 26, 1799.
79	" Phebe Barker,	Oct. 14, 1800.
79	" Lydia,	Sept. 22, 1802.
79	" Mary Tew,	Feb. 20, 1804.
79	" Anna Sprague,	Dec. 23, 1807.
79	" Barbara,	Jan. 3, 1810.
95	" Sally, of Joseph and Eunice,	Nov. 22, 1813.
95	" Henry Tillinghast,	April 6, 1815.
134	" Cynthia Peckham, of Gideon and Jane	Oct. 1, 1824.

S

40	SANFORD William Smith, of Giles and Elizabeth,	May 2, 1759.
40	" Sarah,	Dec. 7, 1760.
40	" William Smith, 2d,	June 14, 1762.
40	" Elizabeth,	Jan. 29, 1764.
40	" Richard,	Oct. 9, 1765.
40	" Edward,	Feb. 15, 1767.
40	" Anne,	Feb. 7, 1769.
40	" Giles,	Feb. 15, 1771.
40	" John,	Oct. 26, 1772.
40	" Samnel,	June 14, 1774.
23	SHAW Sarah, of Lemuel and Sarah,	Nov. 19, 1751.
104	SHEFFIELD Nathan R., of Benjamin T. and Mary,	Aug. 7, 1804.
104	" Elisha Barker,	Dec. 14, 1805.
104	" Benjamin Helme,	Jan. 21, 1807.
104	" Juliana,	Feb. 20, 1809.
36	SHELDON Sarah, of Jonathan and Mary,	Jan. 15, 1752.
36	" John,	May 24, 1753.
36	" Jonathan,	Jan. 23, 1757.
115	SHERMAN Abraham, of Walter and Rebecca,	7m., 4th, 1790.
44	" Atherton, of Solomon and Sybel,	Jan. 29, 1791.
44	" Mindsell,	March 15, 1793.
44	" Saunders,	April 10, 1795.
44	" Timothy,	Aug. 21, 1797.
122	" Ann, of Job and Rebecca,	Oct. 16, 1806.
122	" Betsey,	Nov. 11, 1807.
122	" Lavina,	July 4, 1809.
122	" Frances Henderson,	Dec. 16, 1812.
91	SISSON Anne, of Pardon, Jr., and Mary,	Feb. 5, 1799.
91	" Matthew,	Dec. 20, 1800.
58	" Robert Cornell, of David and Rebecca,	May 3, 1800.
58	" Silas,	Feb. 26, 1802.
58	" Adeline,	April 29, 1804.
58	" Henry Tew,	Aug. 29, 1806.
58	" David,	May 30, 1809.
31	SLOCUM Avis, of Peleg and Avis,	June 28, 1739.
54	" Peleg, of John and Catherine,	Aug. 24, 1753.
32	" Avis, of Giles and Mary,	April 5, 1755.
32	" Phebe,	Nov. 13, 1761.
32	" Mary,	Oct. 22, 1764.
32	" Giles,	Jan. 5, 1767.
54	" John, of John and Hannah,	Dec. 20, 1756.
54	" Joseph Wanton,	Nov. 18, 1762.
54	" Rebecca,	July 8, 1765.
54	" Mary,	May 4, 1767.
54	" William Brown,	April 26, 1770.

70	SLOCUM	Caleb Brown, of John, Jr., and Phebe,	Oct. 2, 1779
70	"	Sarah,	March 9, 1786.
70	"	Hannah,	Sept. 15, 1789.
145	"	Sarah, of William and Mary,	April 5, 1786.
145	"	William,	April 23, 1788.
145	"	Mary,	Dec. 21, 1792.
145	"	Gardiner Thurston,	Aug. 3, 1798.
54	"	John Wanton, of Joseph Wanton and Rhoda,	Feb. 11, 1792.
106	"	Phebe, of John and Elizabeth,	Jan. 16, 1797.
106	"	Holder,	June 2, 1799.
106	"	Jonathan S., (also recorded on page 115),	June 7, 1802.
145	"	Mary Jane, of Gardiner T. and Eliza,	Feb. 25, 1825.
145	"	Alice Sherman,	Sept 29, 1826.
145	"	Sarah Catherine,	March 25, 1829.
145	"	Margaret Amelia,	March 25, 1829.
145	"	William F.,	May 2, 1833.
145	"	Emeline Randall,	Feb. 16, 1836.
145	"	Julia Ann P.,	Sept. 17, 1838.
1	SMITH	Edward, of Elisha and Ssrah,	Jan. 7, 1730.
1	"	Elijah,	Nov. 10, 1732.
1	"	Peleg,	March 31, 1735.
1	"	Elizabeth,	Nov. 20, 1736.
1	"	Isaac,	May 2, 1739.
1	"	Philip,	Dec. 12, 1741.
1	"	Hope,	Jan. 12, 1744.
14	"	Rachel, of Henry and Rachel,	July 26, 1742.
14	"	Sarah,	(sic) Feb. 29, 1743.
14	"	William,	Jan. 12, 1746.
14	"	Elizabeth,	Jan. 10, 1747.
23	"	Isaac, of Edward and Sarah	Aug. 2, 1751.
27	"	Elizabeth,	Aug. 6, 1753.
61	"	Philip, of Benjamin and Elizabeth,	Oct. 22, 1753.
61,68	"	John,	March 10, 1760.
173	"	Peleg, died in his 75th year,	Feb. 10, 1760.
60	"	Sarah, of Philip and Sarah,	Dec. 25, 1764.
60	"	George,	Nov. 20, 1766.
60	"	Edward,	Sept. 26, 1768.
60	"	Elisha,	July 9, 1770.
88	"	William, of John and Henrietta,	March 8, 1783.
142	"	Benjamin Whitehead,	Aug. 31, 1784.
142	"	Mary,	April 16, 1786.
142	"	John,	May 15, 1788.
173	"	John, son of Benjamin, died in his 28th year,	Feb. ——, 1788.
142	"	Abigail, of Edward and Henrietta,	March 2, 1790.
142	"	Nancy,	March 13, 1794.
142	"	Ruth,	July 13, 1796.
142	"	Phebe,	May 18, 1801.
142	"	Abner,	Dec. 23, 1802.
142	"	Clarissa,	March 7, 1803.
142	"	Edwin,	May 15, 1805.
142	"	Rachel,	March 25, 1807.
90	"	John Easton, of Edward and Hannah,	Jan. 26, 1792.
100	"	Sarah, of George and Rebecca,	Aug. 16, 1797.
100	"	Isaac,	Sept. 8, 1799.
100	"	William,	Dec. 31, 1801.
100	"	Adaline,	Jan. 13, 1805.
18	"	Harriet H., of Elisha and Polly,	Nov. 12, 1798.
174	"	Benjamin, died in his 77th year,	Jan. 9, 1799.
108	"	Malinda, of William and Mary,	Oct. 24, 1805.
108	"	Simeon,	Dec. 14, 1806.
108	"	Raymond,	Nov. 14, 1809.
108	"	Abbert,	Oct. 12, 1811.
108	"	John,	Jan. 28, 1814.
132	"	Isaiah, of George and Rebecca,	Oct. 5, 1807.
132	"	David,	June 14, 1814.

132	SMITH	Rebecca Barker, of George and Hannah,	June 23, 1821.
132	"	Martha Maria,	April 14, 1823.
132	"	David,	June 7, 1825.
132	"	Hannah Mary,	Feb. 25, 1828.
132	"	George Washington,	March 6, 1832.
174	"	Edward, of Benjamin, died, in his 69th year, June 15, 1824.
174	"	Henrietta, wife of Edward, died, in her 62d year, Aug. 6, 1828.
172	"	Philip, of Benjamin, died, in his 81st year,	July 27, 1834.
172	"	George, died, in his 69th year,	Aug. 22, 1835.
48	STODDARD	Thomas, of Salisbury and Hannah,	June 13, 1751.
48	"	Rachel,	Feb. 4, 1754.
48	"	Isaac,	March 26, 1757.
48	"	Hannah,	June 1, 1760.
48	"	Ruth,	March 11, 1765.
48	"	Salisbury,	May 19, 1767.
48	"	Samuel,	April 19, 1769.
51	"	Mercy, of David and Mary,	Feb. 27, 1761.
51	"	Abigail,	April 16, 1764.
51	"	Arnold,	April 7, 1766.
95	"	Thomas, of Salisbury and Phebe,	Oct. 8, 1792.
113	"	Joseph, of Samuel and Elizabeth,	Nov. 13, 1794.
113	"	Sarah,	Oct. 15, 1796.
113	"	Jonathan,	Oct. 10, 1798.
113	"	William,	Feb. 28, 1801.
113	"	Nathaniel,	Aug. 6, 1803.
113	"	Henry,	Sept. 5, 1806.
113	"	Elizabeth,	May 10, 1809.
75	SWEET	Oliver, of George and Mary,	Dec. 14, 1802.
75	"	Benjamin,	March 26, 1804.
75	"	George,	Jan. 6, 1806.
75	"	Albert,	March 10, 1808.
75	"	Mary Whitman,	May 1, 1809.
125	"	Almira, of Oliver and Sarah,	June 27, 1823.
125	"	Ambrose W.,	July 22, 1827.
125	"	Maria A.,	April 4, 1830.
125	"	Charles G.,	Feb. 25, 1832.
125	"	Mary A. F.,	Jan. 28, 1836.

T

150	TAGGART	Clarke, of Capt. William and Mary,	Jan. 27, 1759.
150	"	Mary, wife of Clarke,	Sept. 12, 1763.
150	"	James, of Clarke and Mary,	Sept. 12, 1783.
150	"	John,	Aug. 8, 1786.
150	"	Mary,	July 12, 1789.
150	"	Thomas,	April 27, 1791.
150	"	Joseph,	Oct. 8, 1793.
150	"	Ruth,	Oct. 8, 1793.
150	"	Ruth, 2d.,	March 15, 1797.
141	"	Joseph Wanton, of William and Sarah Anne,	Aug. 30, 1823.
141	"	Benjamin Franklin,	March 31, 1826.
141	"	Elizabeth Wyatt,	April 27, 1829.
141	"	William Gammell,	Sept. 19, 1837.
5	TAYLOR	Robert, of John and Judith,	July 13, 1719.
5	"	Judith,	Feb. 13, 1720.
177	"	Robert above died	Oct. 25, 1721.
5	"	Robert, 2d.,	July 3, 1725.
5	"	Mary,	July 16, 1727.
5	"	John,	July 21, 1729.
5	"	Deborah,	Dec. 27, 1731.
5	"	Freelove,	April 24, 1733.
177	"	Robert, of John and Mary, died, aged about 2 months, Aug. 27, 1725.	
177	"	John, of John and Mary, died, aged 12 days,	Oct. 3, 1729.

9	TEW	Henry, of Henry and Sarah,	Feb. 14, 1735.
9	"	Ann,	Feb. 11, 1737.
9	"	Job,	Jan. 9, 1739.
9	"	Mary,	Dec. 14, 1742.
9	"	Admiral,	July 26, 1745.
24	"	Edward, of Edward and Mary,	March 13, 1746.
24	"	Mary,	Jan. 21, 1747-8.
50	TRIPP	John, of Job and Hannah,	Sept. 5, 1766.

U

17	UPHAM	Anne, of Edward and Sarah,	April 6, 1750.
24	"	Asaph,	June 29, 1752.
31	"	James,	Jan. 29, 1755.
35	"	George,	Aug. 20, 1757.
35	"	Mary,	Nov. 15, 1761.

V

111	VARS	John, of Christopher and Sarah,	Jan. 12, 1810.
111	"	Elizabeth,	May 30, 1811.

W

29	WEAVER	Christopher, of Benjamin and Deborah,	April 30, 1741.
29	"	Deborah,	Aug. 23, 1742.
29	"	Joseph,	May 7, 1744.
29	"	Jonathan,	April 23, 1746.
29	"	Benjamin,	May 28, 1748.
29	"	James,	April 28, 1750.
29	"	Mary,	June 28, 1752.
29	"	Coggeshall,	June 5, 1754.
4	"	Joseph, of Benjamin, Jr., and Deborah,	May 11, 1744.
28	"	Mary, of Clement, Jr., and Rosanna,	Jan. 30, 1745-6.
28	"	Elizabeth,	May 7, 1748.
28	"	John,	Sept. 14, 1750.
28	"	Stephen,	Jan. 10, 1753.
28	"	Daniel,	April 18, 1755.
28	"	Matthew,	
10, 30	"	Joseph, of Thomas (of Benjamin) and Ann,	Nov. 29, 1746.
30	"	Jacob,	Nov. 22, 1748.
30	"	Jacob,	d. Aug. 31, 1754.
30	"	Hannah,	July 26, 1750.
30	"	Benjamin,	Feb. 3, 1754.
30	"	Perry,	May 5, 1755.
20	"	Sarah, of Thomas (of Thomas, Jr.) and Mary,	May 2, 1750.
22, 49	"	Elizabeth, of William and Content,	June 27, 1751.
27, 49	"	Job,	Feb. 18, 1754.
49	"	Ruth,	Feb. 25, 1757.
49	"	James,	July 28, 1759.
49	"	Wait,	Jan. 30, 1762.
49	"	Robert,	June 14, 1766.
24	"	Mercy, of Thomas (of Thomas, Jr.) and Mary,	July 1, 1752.
30	"	Patience,	Feb. 16, 1754.
30	"	Mercy,	
29	"	Robert, of Thomas and Alice,	Sept. 12, 1756.
29	"	Mary,	Aug. 9, 1758.
29	"	Thomas,	Feb. 23, 1760.
29	"	Abigail,	April 11, 1762.
29	"	Walter,	Sept. 16, 1764.
37	"	Hannah, of James and Rebecca,	Nov. 11, 1756.
37	"	Mary,	March 1, 1759.
37	"	Gideon,	Aug. 27, 1752.
37	"	Samuel, of Thomas, Jr., and Mary,	June 15, 1758.

87	WEAVER Mary, of Thomas, Jr., and Mary,	July 18, 1760.
87	" Hannah.	Oct. 1. 1762.
87	" Thomas.	Oct. 11. 1763.
87	" Rebecca.	July 10, 1766.
47	" Abigail, of Thomas (of Clement) and Alice,	Nov. 6. 1766.
47	" Holmes.	July 24, 1769.
47	" Timothy,	June 29, 1772.
47	" Mary,	Sept. 8, 1775.
65	" John, of John and Mary,	Sept. 20. 1768.
87	" Caleb, of Thomas and Mary,	Jan. 2. 1771.
118	" Parker, of Matthew and Susanna,	July 31, 1784.
118	" Lydia, of Parker and Lydia,	June 28, 1810.
118	" Mary Ann,	March 29. 1812.
118	" Thomas Manchester.	April 8. 1814.
118	" John Rogers.	Nov. 16. 1816.
118	" Benjamin Brown.	Feb. 16. 1820.
118	" Mercy.	Sept. 12, 1822.
118	" Stephen,	Dec. 9. 1826.
118	" Marcy,	Nov. 7, 1832.
118	". Parker Hall,	April 26, 1830.
52	" Benoni, of Hannah,	Oct. 23, 1786.
60	" Thomas Coggeshall, of Benoni and Mary,	Sept. 28, 1815.
60	" David Lewis,	Sept. 30, 1817.
60	" Benoni,	Oct. 15, 1819.
60	" Hannah Mary,	Nov. 22, 1820.
60	" Stephen Perry,	Sept 10, 1822.
60	" Joseph Coggeshall,	May 11, 1826.
60	" William Nelson,	Sept. 29, 1827.
60	" Freeborn Coggeshall,	Dec. 18, 1831.
170	" Alton, of Daniel and Caroline C.,	Feb. 24, 1838.
18	WEEDEN Phebe of Jonathan and Mary; (also 21),	Sept. 12, 1750.
18	" Robert,	Oct. 20, 1752.
18	" Christian,	July 20, 1754.
18	" Elizabeth,	Sept. 7, 1760.
18	" William,	Sept. 20, 1763.
18	" Jonathan,	May 5, 1767.
41	" Barbara, of William and Sarah,	Jan. 10, 1740.
41	" Barbara,	d. Oct. 18, 1753.
41	" Hannah,	Nov. 5, 1742.
41	" Joseph,	April 22, 1749.
41	" Christian,	Nov. 25, 1751.
41	" Christian,	d. Oct. 29, 1753.
41	" Sarah,	Nov. 3, 1754.
41	" Peleg,	Feb. 8, 1756.
39	WELLES Wealthian, of Gideon and Wealthian,	Jan. 1, 1759.
32	WHITING Mary, of Amos and Lucretia,	July 16, 1756.
63	WILCOX Samuel Wilbour, of Josiah and Sarah,	Jan. 12, 1768.
63	" Rodman,	March 5, 1770.
63	" Anne,	April 30, 1772.
63	" Josiah,	June 23, 1774.
63	" Sarah, of Josiah and Hannah.	Aug. 23, 1795.
15	WOOD Elizabeth, of Gersham and Sarah,	Jan. 4, 1748-9.
99	" Elizabeth, of John and Mary,	Feb. 1, 1748.
99	" Sarah,	Jan. 22, 1753.
82	WYATT Sarah, of Samuel and Ann,	May 2, 1777.
82	" Elizabeth,	Aug. 31, 1779.
82	" David.	Dec. 19, 1781.
82	" Nathaniel,	Dec. 5, 1787.
121	" Thomas Coggeshall, of David and Ruth.	Aug. 3, 1805.
121	" Ruth Ann,	June 3, 1808.
121	" David Alvin, of David and Jane,	Dec. 12, 1822.
121	" Alanson Peckham,	Oct. 22, 1824.
132	" Ruth Coggeshall, of Thomas C. and Silvester,	Dec. 31, 1825.
132	" Theodore Foster,	Dec. 19, 1828.
132	" Charles Anthony,	March 17, 1836.

Note—Nothing recorded under letters X Y Z.

INDEX.

MIDDLETOWN.

I

Names Occurring in Their Natural Order.

Marriages commence with page 5; births and deaths, page 21.

A

Albro, 5 21.
Allen, 5 21 22.
Almy, 5.
Anthony, 5 22.
Antunes, 6 22.

B

Bailey, 6 22.
Barker, 6 7 22 23 24 25.
Battey, 7.
Beebe, 7.
Billington, 7.
Bliss, 7 25.
Borden, 7.
Bowler, 7.
Brief, 7.
Brownell, 7.
Browning, 7.
Brown, 7 8 25 26.
Buffum, 26.
Burgess, 8.
Burns, 8.
Burroughs, 8.

C

Card, 8 26.
Carpenter, 8.
Carr, 8.
Chapman, 8 26.
Chase, 8 26 27.
Cheeseman, 8.
Church, 8 27.
Clarke, 8 9 27 28.
Clark, 9.
Coggeshall, 9 10 28 29.
Cook, 10.
Cornell, 10 29.
Cory, 10.
Crandall, 10.
Cranston, 10.
Croade, 10.
Crowsher, 10.

D

Davenport, 10.
Davis, 10.
Dawley, 10 29.
Dennis, 10.
Devant, 10.
Dewry, 10.
Dillingham, 10 29.
Dring, 10 29.
Durfee, 10 29 30.
Dyer, 10 11 30.

E

Earl, 11.
Easton, 11 30.
Eddy, 11 30.
Ennis, 11.

F

Fish, 11.
Fones, 11.
Freeborn, 11 30.

G

Gardner, 11 30 31.
Gibbs, 11.
Gifford, 11.
Gould, 11 12 31.
Granger, 12.
Greene, 12 31.
Greenman, 12.

H

Hall, 12 31.
Harrington, 12.
Harris, 12.
Havens, 12.
Hazard, 12.
Head, 12.
Heffernan, 12.

Hoar, 12 31.
Holmes, 31.
Hopkins, 12 31.
Howard, 12.
Howland, 12.
Hunt, 12.

I

Irish, 12 31.

J

Jones, 13.
Joslin, 13.
Josselyn, 13.

K

Kempton, 13.
Kirby, 31.

L

Lake, 13 32.
Larkin, 13.
Lawton, 13.
Lewis, 13.
Little, 13 32.
Luther, 13.

M

Macomber, 13.
Manchester, 13 32 33.
Martin, 13 33.
Mason, 13.
Maxon, 13.
Mitchell, 14 33.
Mishier, 14.

N

Nason, 14.
Negas, 14.

Nichols, 14 33.
Northrup, 14.

O P

Palmer, 14.
Peabody, 14 33 34.
Peckham, 14 15 34 35
  36 37.
Pendleton, 37.
Perry, 15 37.
Phillips, 15 37.
Pitman, 15 37.

Q R

Reed, 37.
Rice, 16 37.
Robertson, 16.
Rogers, 16 37.
Russell, 16.
Ryder, 16 37 38.

S

Sanford, 16 38.
Seager, 16.
Shaw, 16 38.
Sheffield, 16 38.

Sheldon, 16 38.
Sherman, 16 38.
Shrieves, 16.
Sisson, 16 38.
Slocum, 16 17 38 39.
Smith, 17 39 40.
Spooner, 17.
Sprague, 17.
Stoddard, 17 40.
Strange, 17.
Sullings, 17.
Sweet, 18 40.
Sylvester, 18.

T

Taber, 18.
Taggart, 18 40.
Taylor, 18 40.
Tew, 18 41.
Thompkins, 18.
Tompkins, 18.
Torrey, 18.
Tripp, 18 41.
Tucker, 18.
Turner, 18.

U

Upham, 41.

V

Vars, 18 41.
Vickery, 18.

W

Wales, 19.
Ward, 19.
Weaver, 19 41 42.
Weeden, 19 42.
Weekes, 19.
Welles, 19 42.
Wells, 19.
Whitcher, 19.
White, 20.
Whiting, 20 42.
Whitman, 20.
Wilbour, 20.
Wilcox, 20 42.
Wightman, 20.
Wilson, 20.
Woodman, 20.
Wood, 20 42.
Wyatt, 20 42.

X Y Z

II.

Names Occurring Promiscuously.

A

Adlam, 8 10.
Allen, 7 12 19 20.
Almy, 8 19.
Anthony, 9.

B

Bailey, 15 16.
Barker, 8 10 11 12 16
  17 18 28.
Barrows, 7 8 14 15 19
  20.
Billings, 10 20.
Bliss, 5 9 10 11 12 13
  14 16 17.
Borden, 17.
Bradley, 15.
Brown, 11.
Burroughs, 13.

C

Callender, 19.
Choules, 10.
Clarke, 13.
Coggeshall, 9 11.
Cook, 5.
Coon, 14.
Cornell, 5.
Cory, 5 13 15.
Culver, 5.

D

Dehan, 11.
Durfee, 14 19 20.

E

Easton, 6 9 10 11.
Eddy, 5 6 7 8 9 10 11
  12 13 14 15 16 17
  18 19 20.
Ellis, 5.
Estes, 5.
Evert, 15.
Eyres, 6 7 8 14 19.

F

Fisher, 18.

G

Gammell, 17.
Gardiner, 6 12 13 16.
Gibson, 7 12 14 18.
Gorten, 14.
Gould, 6 9 11 13 14 15
  16 19 20.
Graves, 11.

H

Hall, 30.

Hathaway, 10.
Helme, 17 18.
Howard, 8 11 17.

I J K

Kelley, 17 20.

L

Lawton, 14 19.
Leaver, 17.
Lewis, 9.

M

Macumber, 7.
Mason, 6.
McKensie, 18.
Miner, 16.

N

Nichols, 11.
Northup, 10.

O

Othman, 8.

P

Patten, 5 12.
Peabody, 5 6 10 13 18.

III.

Names of Places.

www.ingramcontent.com/pod-product-compliance
Lightning Source LLC
Chambersburg PA
CBHW060558100426
42742CB00013B/2605